Georgian
LIVERPOOL

Georgian LIVERPOOL

HUGH HOLLINGHURST

AMBERLEY

Cunard 'Britannia' class paddle steamer on service to Halifax, Canada, at the end of the Georgian era.

First published 2023

Amberley Publishing
The Hill, Stroud
Gloucestershire, GL5 4EP

www.amberleybooks.com

British Library Cataloguing in Publication Data.
A catalogue record for this book is available from the British Library.

ISBN 978 1 3981 1063 2 (paperback)
ISBN 978 1 3981 1064 9 (ebook)

Typeset in 10pt on 13pt Sabon.
Typesetting by SJmagic DESIGN SERVICES, India.
Printed in the UK.

CONTENTS

Typical Georgian doorway, fanlight and windows.

ACKNOWLEDGEMENTS

To the following for illustrations:

Carol Young page 92

David Hearn and Richard Jackson (TheDustyTeapot Publications) pages 9, 15, 16, 17, 24, 28, 38, 40, 42, 43, 45, 46, 53, 54, 61, 67

Jane Mellor pages 24, 29(2), 47, 51, 57, 60, 73

John Haslam page 50

Liverpool Record Office pages 10, 17, 18, 21 (2), 22, 27, 30, 35, 44, 54, 55, 69, 71, 76

Paul Breen pages 4, 14, 15, 20, 26, 31, 34, 37, 52, 60, 62, 68, 74

Other photographs were taken by Paul Hollinghurst or the author. Other images are from the author's collection.

Above all, I pay tribute as always to my wife Joan for her encouragement, support, patience and understanding.

INTRODUCTION

Georgian Liverpool started, and ended, with two events that shaped the course of history – for the town, the country and the whole world. The year after the accession of George I in 1714, work started on the first commercial enclosed wet dock, while in 1830, the same year as the death of George IV, the first inter-city railway service was instituted from Liverpool to Manchester. In between, the architecture of the town followed an engaging progression of overlapping styles, which culminated in the grand neoclassical terraces, churches and public buildings of the late eighteenth and early nineteenth centuries.

The construction of the original Old Dock led to an exponential rise in commercial prosperity. This was driven by the infamous triangular trade route: goods exported from Liverpool to Africa were bartered for slaves in Africa who were transported to America. Cotton and sugar were then brought back to Liverpool on the home run. Proceeds were spent on building projects and charitable purposes for which the profiteers were praised and memorialised. By 1764 Liverpool had overtaken Bristol, its greatest rival in the slave trade, with well over double the number of sailings inwards and outwards (1,598), many of them to Africa and from America. However, opposition to the slave trade in the 1790s led to its abolition in 1807 and cotton became the main trade through the town.

Liverpool increasingly became a magnet for many thousands of aspiring or despairing English, Welsh, Scots and Irish. Between the start and end of the eighteenth century, Liverpool's population increased elevenfold from about 7,000 to 77,000 and then doubled by 1830. Overcrowding led to the construction of low-grade housing and widespread poverty. However, 'merchant palaces' also reflected the growing affluence of the town. Such was the scale of two of these, the Royal Institution and Blackburne House, that they became and have survived as educational institutions. Two more, the Blue Coat School, the oldest building still standing in the centre of Liverpool, and the Mechanics Institute in a different form, still bear witness to a desire to preserve and improve the quality of educational and social life in the town. The resources to fund these projects stemmed ultimately from the continual improvement and extension of the dock system. From the opening of the second, Salthouse, dock in 1753 until 1832 the system was enlarged fifteen-fold with increasing complexity. Of the public buildings, the Exchange, opened in 1803, was described in the words of a gushing guidebook of the period as 'the finest commercial building in the empire'. Promotion of the arts and sciences was championed by polymath William Roscoe and the Rathbone family. The Athenaeum, Royal Institution, and Lyceum and Union Libraries were all founded within the space of five years. Enthusiasm for the theatre led to riots when attendance was threatened. Churches ranged from early Georgian simplicity to neoclassical grandeur at the end of the period. The many Roman Catholic and Nonconformist buildings reflected the cosmopolitan population of fascinating and formative Georgian Liverpool.

Liverpool Work House or House of Correction.

1
COMMERCE

Old Dock and Fourth Custom House

The Old Dock was opened in 1715, the year after the accession of George I ushered in the Georgian era. It was the first commercial enclosed wet dock, a town-changing, and indeed a world-changing, event. Liverpool merchants took on a huge financial risk which was amply repaid after ten years of great courage and persistence.

Old Dock and Fourth Custom House around 1750.

The innovation resonates to this day. In 1701 only one ship (called the *Blessing*) out of 374 sailed from Liverpool to Africa; in 1730 fifteen out of 412 and in 1771 106 out of 819. This involved the transportation of slaves from Africa to America on the infamous triangular route. Goods were carried from Britain to Africa, slaves from there to America, cotton back home, a practice in which very few merchants and their associates were untainted. It enabled Liverpool to draw ahead of Bristol as the second port in the land after London. Liverpool's Fourth Custom House was built around 1700. The owner of the *Blessing* was Thomas Earle, founder of a dynasty that made huge profits from slavery.

The Old Dock is on the right of the illustration, St Thomas's Church tower in the centre and on the left the Fourth Custom House flying St George's flag. The Custom House was entered by a flight of steps through arches which led to a piazza, off which offices could be accessed and a long room on the first floor.

A century later, the dock, outgrowing its usefulness, was filled in and the magnificent Fifth Custom House was constructed on the site. Today, the remains of the Old Dock can be seen through a window in the pavement and visited underground.

Map of Liverpool, 1720

In founding the first royal borough on Merseyside, King John laid out a simple plan for Liverpool as can be seen in the map of 1720 (orientated to the east). The basic

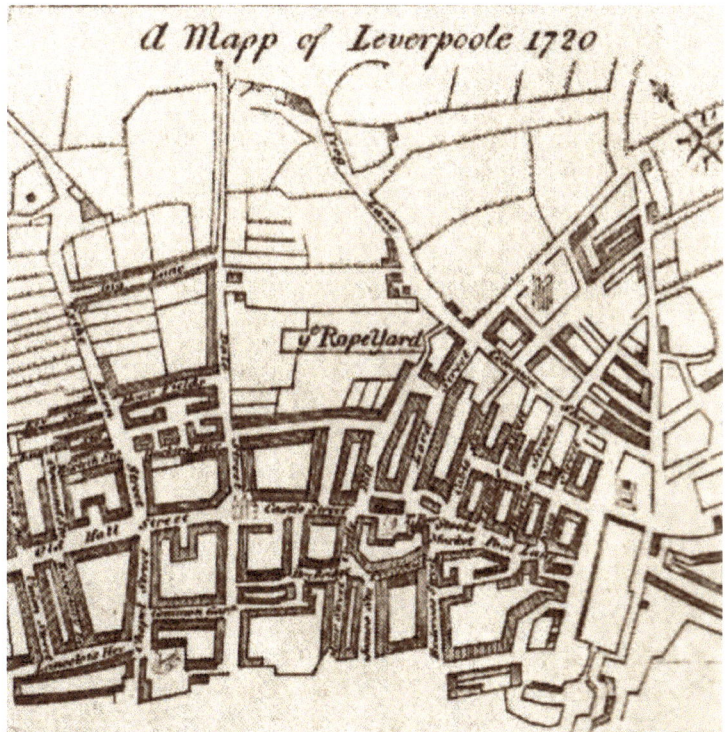

'A Map of Leverpoole 1720'.

design was in the form of the letter H. The left-hand (northern) side was formed by Tythe Barn (now Tithebarn) Street and Chapel Street leading down to St Nicholas' Church (pictured). The crosspiece is formed by Old Hall Street and the right-hand side by Dale Street and Water Street. The Town Hall is pictured at the junction between these last three from where Castle Street leads to the Castle and Pool Lane from there to the Old Dock. Lord Street leads off to the east with its extension, Church Street, not named but with St Peter's pictured by it.

Salthouse Dock

The Old Dock, groundbreaking as it was, quickly became a victim of its own success and proved incapable of handling the increase in traffic that it created. The Salthouse Dock, taking fifteen years to construct and opened in 1753, more than doubled the capacity of the port. The site of the dock was determined by the need to service the salt works of John Blackburne near to the Old Dock but it was soon crowded with vessels of general trade and in 1793 the salt works were moved to Garston. It is the oldest surviving dock and the accompanying photo indicates subsequent development. The corner of the Albert Dock can be seen on the immediate left. Behind the tall buildings on the left is the site of the Old Dock and in front of them, hidden from view, Canning Dock, second to be opened. King's and Queen's Docks behind the viewer are now filled in.

Salthouse Dock in 2016.

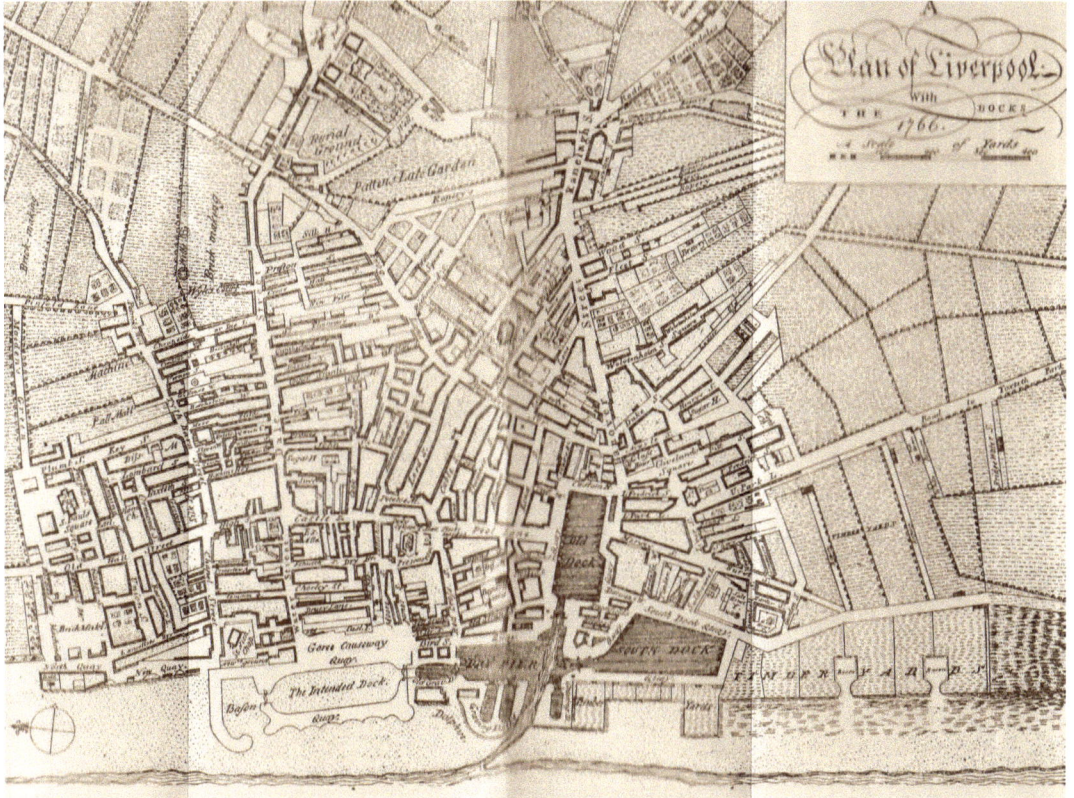

Williamson's Plan of Liverpool with the docks, 1766.

Map of Liverpool, 1766

The map is orientated from the west as usual at the time. The shaded docks are a prominent feature. The Old Dock is furthest inland, the South Dock (later Salthouse) to the right and the Dry Pier (later Canning Dock) to the left. 'The Intended Dock' to the left of that is George's Dock, later filled in to build the 'Three Graces'. Top right, the roperies are a prominent feature (now Bold Street).

George's Dock

The third dock to be built was George's, completed in 1771. It occupied the site on which the 'Three Graces' were built when the dock was filled in later in 1900. It thus formed the basis for George's Stage, which, added to the Prince's Stage to the north, later grew into a half-mile landing stage. The view of the 1840s shows paddle steamers, which first arrived on the Mersey from the Clyde in 1815, to ply between Liverpool and Runcorn. They are moored by the departure point for most of the ferries for the

George's Dock and Pier Head in 1844.

Wirral. The Birkenhead shore can be seen on the far right in the distance with the river and sky punctuated by the masts of sailing ships. The tower of George's baths can be seen to the left of the flagpole and on the far left are the masts of ships moored in George's Dock. The two rounded buildings were shelters.

Goree Warehouses

Liverpool's extensive growth during the eighteenth century, due in large measure to profits made in the Atlantic slave trade, brought an increasing demand for storage space. In response to this, in 1793 successful merchants built the Goree Warehouses, larger than the celebrated warehouses of Antwerp and Venice. Significantly, they were named after Senegal's Goree Islands off the coast of Africa, a great slave trading centre. That year a financial crisis, triggered by the start of the Napoleonic War, engulfed Liverpool and was saved only by the town printing its own bank notes. Worse followed in 1802, when a fire, said to be the greatest in the British dominions since the Great Fire of London, destroyed the Goree buildings with its merchandise from abroad, such as sugars, rum, coffee, cotton, tallow, hemp and grain. Only the chance of a favourable wind and high tide enabled ships in the Old Dock to scramble for safety in the river. The damage, £323.000 (over £11 million today), bankrupted the fire insurance company. No lives were lost except for a man killed in superintending the levelling of the debris and 'as he was an old servant of the Corporation, they generously allowed his widow a pension'. The ruins smouldered for three months and burning flakes and sparks were carried far and wide across the country in every direction.

The replacement for the warehouses was completed in 1810 and trade with Africa continued after Parliament brought an end to the British slave trade. Great care was taken over its construction. which acted as a model for warehouses for the next fifty

Above: Goree Warehouses in 1810.

Right: Goree Warehouses, George's Quay and James Street in 1844.

years. Standard clauses were included in future contracts governing height, building lines, materials and their duration. The new Goree warehouses were built of brick, only six storeys high, when many of the others were over thirteen. Also included was provision for arcades at ground level (known as Goree Piazza) to protect pedestrians with offices and shops behind. However, developers were reluctant to adopt these superior specifications, involving as they did extra expense without benefit to themselves, and they were eventually discontinued.

The warehouses are straight ahead as viewed in 1844 from the George's Baths. The low bridge in the centre crosses the cut, which enabled the ships from George's Dock on the left to reach the Mersey through the Canning Dock behind the building on the right. Behind James Street in the centre rises the tower of St George's Church. The warehouses survived until after the Second World War when they were demolished following war damage. Conveniently for the urban planners this eased the passage for north/south traffic and made possible one side of the proposed ring road later on.

King's and Queen's Docks

After the building of George's Dock in 1771, trade flourished in spite of the American War of Independence. By the time the construction of the King's and Queen's Docks was authorised in 1785 the number of ships using the port had increased by 60 per cent. The complex added a massive 14 acres of wet docks with graving docks as well, and the whole system was completed by 1796. An imposing tobacco warehouse of two storeys was built as illustrated. It was graced by a pediment above the central entrance and a cupola above. Bulls eye windows distinguished the bays at either end. Measuring 210 feet by 180 feet, it was intended to hold 7,000 hogsheads (barrels) of tobacco, each weighing about 1,000 pounds. Erected by the Corporation, it was rented out to the government for being an excellent preventative against theft and smuggling. It barely lasted twenty years and was replaced by a gigantic structure (577 feet by 241 feet) capable of containing 23,000 hogsheads.

 The docks have been filled in and the site redeveloped, most notably for the Arena and Conference Centre. The warehouse was demolished in 1904 with the storage of tobacco transferred to the gargantuan warehouse in Stanley Dock, now being converted into nearly 500 apartments.

King's Dock Warehouse in 1810.

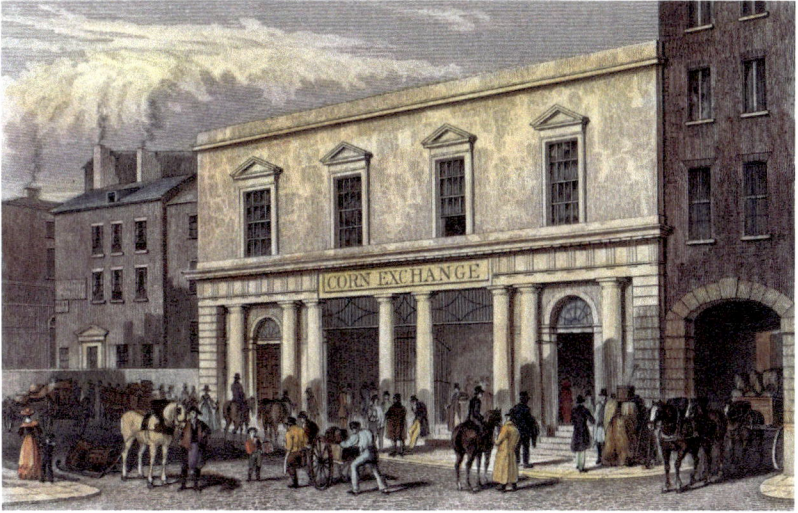

Corn
Exchange.

Corn Exchange

At the start of the nineteenth century, corn merchants travelled from warehouse to warehouse to inspect the corn and conclude a bargain. They met outside the old Exchange and, when the new Exchange was built, they felt the need for one of their own. A dedicated corn exchange would save them a lot of time, trouble and expense. There, they could inspect samples from the different warehouses. It was objected that they would still have to travel to the warehouse to be sure that the corn was as sampled. However, it was pointed out that a corn exchange would in most cases need only one journey, not several, to be assured of this. So, a hundred subscribers contributed a hundred shares of a hundred pounds, each worth £10,000 today. The best architect of the town at the time, John Foster Senior ('King of Liverpool'), was engaged to design a building that satisfied the requirements of the trade and presented an image of investing in a prosperous enterprise. It was opened in Brunswick Street in 1807 (the year the Abolition of Slavery Act was passed), conveniently situated for the docks and the new Exchange. A further increase in trade led to a rebuild on a grander scale in 1851, but this was destroyed during the Blitz.

St John's Market

Opened in 1822, the market stood as a prototype for many other market halls throughout the provinces. The walls were formed from 136 stone-trimmed classical arched window bays. They enclosed a covered space 183 yards in length and 45 yards breadth, about the average size of an international football pitch. Four rows of cast-iron pillars (116 in all) divided the interior into five avenues that corresponded to different commodities of food and each avenue was lined with stalls. The roofs over

St John's Market looking towards St Luke's Church in the distance.

two of the avenues were raised above the others to provide a clerestory with a row of windows that illuminated and ventilated the market below. At night, the market was gas-lit, allowing for the working classes to do their shopping. Audubon, the American bird artist who visited it in 1826, comments that it was the finest market he had ever seen and that it was so well lit that he could plainly see the colours of the irises of live pigeons in cages at 10 o'clock at night. Its engineering was ahead of its time: constant water was available from four cast-iron pumps served by underground wells. Decaying through neglect, the market was demolished in 1965 and replaced by a brutalist monstrosity.

Swire's Map of 1823–24

The dotted line shows the built-up area in the 1766 map, indicating the rate of growth in less than sixty years. From left to right (north to south) the enclosed docks are Prince's, George's, Dry (later, Canning), Old, Salthouse, King's and Queen's. Bottom left is the distinctive horseshoe shape of the prison with the sinuous curve of the Leeds Liverpool canal winding past it. Halfway between that and the Old Dock is the outline of the H pattern of the seven ancient streets (see 1720 map). The crosspiece of the H is marked by the Town Hall half enclosed by the Exchange. In the centre of the map is a cluster of major buildings with a large open space appearing as white, now occupied by St George's Hall and St John's Gardens. The open space included the Haymarket,

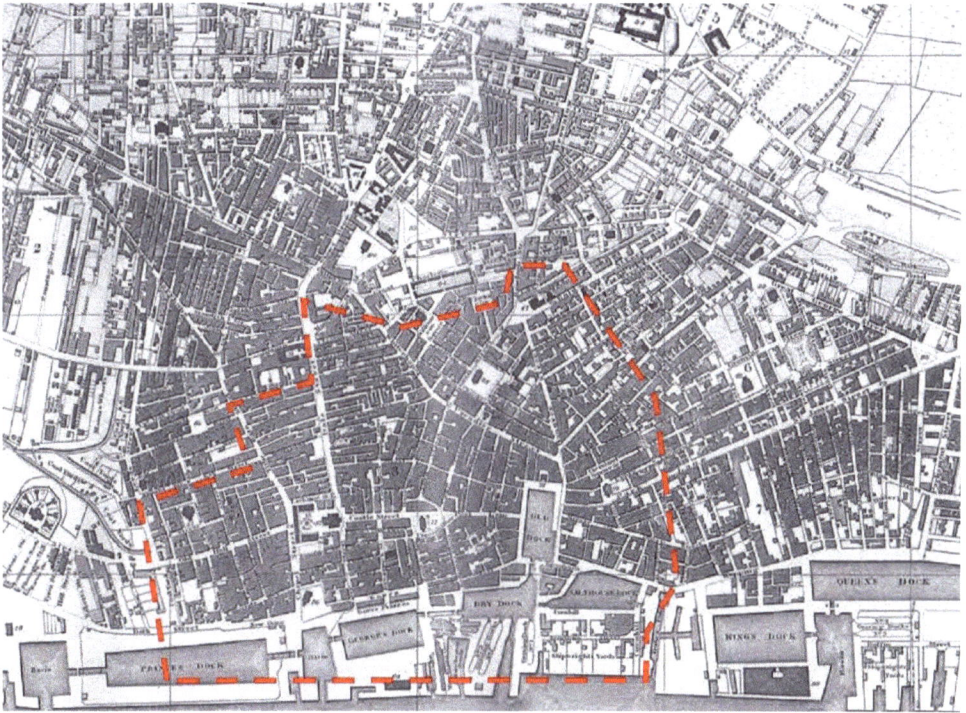

Swire's map of 1823–24.

Islington and Scotland Road Markets. In this downtown area, nearby could be found the Blind Asylum, Christ Church, the Circus, Friends Meeting House, Lunatic Asylum, Old Infirmary, Seamen's Hospital, St John's Church, St Stephen's Church and Baptist, Independent, Methodist and Unitarian Chapels.

Fifth Custom House

The fifth custom house was a prestige project for the town, the architect and the country. In 1826 the Corporation offered the original Old Dock for the site, and John Foster Junior was asked to prepare plans to be presented to the Treasury, who funded the project. Although the foundation stone was laid in 1828, it was not opened for business until 1838. There was opposition from trade unions and master craftsmen, the foundations of the Old Dock on the site caused difficulties, and the stone had to be produced on a huge scale. The main elevation faced the Town Hall along the length of Castle Street to the north as shown in the watercolour of 1844. The architect exploited the relationship between the two buildings brilliantly. The Custom House was impressively adorned by an advanced portico with pediment and giant Ionic columns to match the façade of the Town Hall and was also crowned with a conspicuous dome. The west side facing the sea was equally impressive and balanced by a similar one on the opposite (east) side.

Fifth Custom House in 1844.

For many years the grandeur of the Custom House symbolised the importance of Liverpool in the growth of the country's prosperity through its shipping and trade. The building was seriously damaged in the Second Word War but the outer walls still stood and it could have been restored. However, its usefulness had expired and it was demolished to provide work for the unemployed. Its beautifully carved blocks of stone, up to 5 tons in weight, were dumped to bolster up sea defences. Liverpool One now occupies the site.

Moorish Arch

Opened in 1830, the Liverpool & Manchester Railway was the first intercity railway in the world. The Moorish Arch, John Foster Junior's most unusual and mysterious design, marked the entrance to the tunnel that led down into the town. It housed the stationary steam engines that provided the power to haul the trains up by rope on the steep gradients from the freight terminal at Wapping Dock and the passenger terminal at Crown Street. It also provided a bridge from one side of the cutting to the other. The design of the Moorish key-shaped arch was not only eye catching but also prophetic. It hinted at the possibilities and eventual destinations of railway travel, which were to be realised in a transport revolution.

Moorish Arch, 15
September 1830.

The arch was a victim of the railway's success. It was demolished in 1860 to provide a wider line for access to Crown Street station, by then converted to goods operation.

Crown Street Station

This was the first passenger terminus in Liverpool of the railway to Manchester. First-class carriages stand in the first station 'shed' in the world with their passengers in all their finery under the protective colonnade. Second-class passengers cross the unguarded tracks in peril of tripping over the ropes that haul the trains. More dogs than children accompany the adults. A horse-drawn carriage waits to take passengers on into town. Six years later, a new line was constructed from a station at Edge Hill

Crown Street station.

through a 2,240-yard tunnel to a terminus at Lime Street. That station building has a claim to be one of the oldest in the world still in current use. It dates from 1836 just within the Georgian period (if the reign of William IV can be incorporated into it before Queen Victoria came to the throne the following year). Her reign certainly brought in a new architecture, particularly in Liverpool, that swept away much of the buildings of the Georgian era.

Lime Street Station

The design of the station at Lime Street was way in advance of its precursor at Crown Street, incorporating as it did iron for its supporting columns (their capitals decorated in classical style) and glass in its roof. This would have impressed visiting Manchester businessmen who benefited from the two towns' joint enterprise in manufacturing and marketing cotton, an important consideration in the construction of the line. Liverpool merchants had supported the Confederate cause in the American Civil War and eventually cotton would account for 30 per cent of Liverpool's imports and 42 per cent of its exports.

A magnificent screen in front of Lime Street station was also constructed, the first such station façade in the world and setting the style for over a century. It was a fitting climax to the Georgian architecture of Liverpool and exhibits many of its principles and features. The Corporation contributed handsomely to the façade (created by John Foster Junior), which enhanced the importance of the station. Its stately and grandiose design was an early example of monumental commercialism and conspicuous ornamentation which was funded by the municipality.

Lime Street station.

2
PUBLIC
BUILDINGS

Town Hall

In 1749, Sarah Clayton, Liverpool businesswoman and industrialist, visited Bath and met John Wood the outstanding architect of the day. Her favourable report led to the Corporation engaging him to design a building that combined the work of a Town Hall and Exchange. The engraving shows how the ground floor housed the Exchange where merchants could conduct their business round a central courtyard. However, it was dark and confined so merchants preferred to negotiate outside even when a heavy shower threatened. The Town Hall, above the Exchange, consisted of a council room, other public offices and assembly rooms. The Master of the Ceremonies at Bath (then the height of fashion) described one of them as 'grand, spacious and finely illuminated'. Here, a meeting was held once a fortnight for women to dance and play cards. They were 'elegantly accomplished and perfectly well dressed'. The proceedings were regulated by a lady styled 'The Queen' who ruled with 'very absolute power'. In contrast, in 1775 seamen protesting against reduction in their wages attacked the building with cannon.

On the facing southern façade, the ground floor was, appropriately, rustic in appearance with simple brick arches but the upper storey was lavishly decorated. Here, the arches were framed by decorative Corinthian columns and, between their capitals, carvings illustrated Liverpool's wealth. The centre was emphasised with double columns on either side and a pediment filled with carving. An upward gaze culminated in a squared dome topped by an octagonal cupola from which a magnificent view could be enjoyed of the town, the river and Wales beyond. To the side, the eastern front, which formed the entrance to the Exchange, echoed the effect, less emphatically on the ground floor. The west and north sides, hemmed in by other buildings, were plain.

Improvements were already under way when in 1795 the Town Hall and Exchange was gutted by fire (the main water supplies were frozen and the firemen were unable to use their hoses). James Wyatt, an eminent London architect, was commissioned to repair and improve the damage. A triple arched rusticated base (with large blocks of stone) supported a projecting portico with their columns decorated at the top in the elaborate Corinthian style. The squat dome was raised on a drum, shedding greater light on the entrance hall. It was crowned by a female seated figure, which could represent Minerva, the Roman goddess of wisdom, or Britannia, the British goddess of the sea (her shield

Left: Town Hall of 1747 before the fire of 1795.

Below: Town Hall rebuild after the fire of 1795.

incorporates the Union Jack). Liverpool would wish to be associated with either of these figures and many images of them have been created throughout the city. The interior was remodelled for Town Hall purposes with a Council Chamber and offices on the ground floor. The grand staircase rises up from the site of the central open court of the original Exchange. At a half landing stands a statue of George Canning, Member of Parliament for Liverpool from 1812 to 1822, and Prime Minister in 1827 for 119 days. The staircase then divides and turns back on itself to reach the upper storey. There, reception rooms, ballrooms and, most sumptuous of all, a magnificent dining room all display refinement of the highest order to demonstrate the wealth and ambition of late Georgian Liverpool. The accommodation for civic events was hugely increased. To celebrate the reverses of Napoleon in his Russian campaign of 1812, events over a four-day period included a ball for 1,000 guests, a public dinner for 400 and fireworks on the slopes of Edge Hill.

Election hustings and banquets for interested parties used to be held at the Town Hall and victorious candidates were chaired from there to enjoy the acclamations of their victorious supporters. For many years the winners for the two places in parliament had been Tories Bamber Gascoyne and Colonel Banastre Tarleton (a national hero for his exploits in America), who campaigned on a pro-slave trade and 'No Popery' platform. However, in 1806 William Roscoe was persuaded at the last minute to oppose them with a liberal manifesto. Roscoe, a renaissance polymath, was then at the height of his career as a writer, collector of art, botanist and banker. He came out top of the poll: Gascoyne, coming second, was also elected

Town Hall staircase.

View of Town Hall from Dale Street in 1844.

and Tarleton eliminated. As a Member of Parliament in the ensuing year, Roscoe supported the abolition of the slave trade (successfully) and the introduction of a bill to relax the penal laws against Roman Catholics (unsuccessfully) but George III called for fresh elections in 1807. In the previous campaign there had been some rioting and disorder, quelled by the swearing in of special constables and the offer of a reward of 50 guineas (over £4,000 today) for conviction of offenders. However, on this occasion, as soon as Roscoe returned to Liverpool, his welcoming procession was attacked. Horses and their riders were assailed with sticks by men in Tarleton's colours (green) and sailors from the African slave trade. A stone, accompanied by threats, was thrown at Roscoe from the Town Hall, a horse was stabbed with a knife and in the ensuing affray one of his supporters was killed. Roscoe withdrew from the campaign and suffered a humiliating defeat.

The Town Hall stood out amidst the lower buildings of the period and continued to dominate for decades as illustrated in a watercolour of 1844. Now, it is overshadowed by its neighbours, not least by the rebuild of the Exchange Buildings and the neighbouring Martins Bank.

Gaol

This 'magnificent castle', as described by a guide in 1797, certainly gives the impression of great solidity, softened by patterning and a handsome entrance. John Howard, the prison reformer, had given advice on a design for a new gaol in Liverpool based on the recently constructed Newgate prison in London (and gave his name to Great Howard Street on which it eventually stood). It shares monumentality and an expression of

Gaol by Herdman.

retributive justice with Newgate, although not with John Howard's humanitarian ideals. John visited the prison five times in fifteen years to give a dinner to the inmates on Christmas day. It was opened for visitors in 1793 but it was only in 1811 that the prison was used for its original purpose. Until then it had been used to house French prisoners of war. Local residents had been incarcerated in the old tower in Water Street and a house of correction.

When constructed, the prison was in the fields but by the end of the Georgian era it had been surrounded by the growing town. It was pulled down in 1855 when the present prison was built in Walton.

Waterworks

The Berry Street waterworks were extremely important for the general welfare of the town. In the 1700s water was conveyed from pumps in carts for sale at a rate which forced many inhabitants to economise to their discomfort. Now, in 1801, pumps worked by steam engines could force water through pipes to all parts of the town and a levy was made on each house in proportion to its rent. The chimney for the furnaces can be seen in the etching with a magnificent façade, which emphasised the importance of the enterprise. An imposing gateway was flanked by office blocks with typical Georgian windows and porticoes decorated in elaborate classical style. The water came from springs in Bootle that gushed water at the rate of 200 gallons per minute, which was then stored in a reservoir for distribution to the waterworks and other parts of the town. The Berry Street waterworks were financed by a share subscription and run by the Corporation, as was another on Copperas Hill. Two others to the north of the town were managed by a Bootle water company.

Waterworks in 1810.

Further improvements were made in the early part of the nineteenth century, which were later completely transformed by the importation of water from reservoirs in Lancashire and Wales.

Exchange

The ground floor of the Town Hall that was built in 1747 contained provision for an Exchange. The entrance through three arched doorways on the east side of the Town Hall building led to an open square space surrounded by a covered piazza. This was supported by columns in fine classical style but the windows below were described as being 'minced into useless balustrades and the whole garnished with a redundancy of childish ornament'. In spite, or maybe because, of this, business was often conducted as before in the open at the end of Castle Street in front of the Town Hall.

When the building was damaged by fire in 1795, the rebuild contained no provision for the Exchange. The deficiency was remedied in 1803 by the construction of a new Exchange at the back of the Town Hall, completed in 1807. It enclosed the Exchange Flags on three sides, with the north side of the Town Hall making the fourth. Designed by John Foster Senior, it was a prestige building, boasting that it was more than twice as large as its London counterpart. Stone of the highest quality was obtained from the quarries of the Earl of Sefton in Toxteth Park. The lower storey had a rustic finish but Corinthian, the most ornate order of architecture, was chosen to decorate the upper-storey pilasters on all three sides. The columns of the portico at the centre point of the side facing the Town Hall were also Corinthian to match the

Exchange as it appeared before the fire of 1795.

Exchange in 1810.

decoration of the back of the Town Hall opposite. The height of the paired monolithic columns (25 feet) was claimed to be the greatest in England. There was an entrance on each end of the wings that led through to a piazza 15 feet wide surrounding all three sides of the building. This provided shelter for the merchants and enabled them to conduct their business in all weathers. The main entrance in the centre could be accessed either from the Exchange Flags or Old Hall Street. Three open arches led through to a vestibule with thirty-two coupled columns in the plainer Doric order of architecture. The Old Hall Street entrance was not so elaborate as its companion opposite the Town Hall but nevertheless imposing with tall pilasters and overarching pediment. On that side, doors led to warehouse accommodation. The east (far side in the engraving) of the building contained a news/coffee room as illustrated and a room above it for underwriters on the principle of Lloyds in London. The newsroom, measuring 94 feet by 52 feet and 31 feet high, was the hub of the Exchange and occupied most of the lower storey. Two rows of monolithic Ionic columns (decorated with scrolls at the top) 21 feet high formed an imposing colonnade and supported a coved ceiling with decorated panels.

Unfortunately, the wings of the Exchange were hemmed in by other buildings and the whole obscured by the Town Hall. However, the scheme did create the open space of the Exchange Flags, which survives to this day. There were those who thought at the time that an opportunity had been missed for creating an axis from the Town Hall towards an Exchange on the site of the Old Dock. This vista was later fulfilled by John Foster Junior's Custom House instead. At the time, an extension of the route beyond to Park Lane and St James's Street was imagined from which beautiful views could have been enjoyed both ways but the opportunity was lost.

Exchange Newsroom.

Foster's buildings were demolished, and lamented, in 1862 to make way for a second Exchange in a Flemish Renaissance style to be demolished in its turn for the present plain and uninspiring 1930s building.

George III Statue

The foundation stone of the statue of George III was laid with great celebration on the 50th anniversary of his accession on 25 October 1809. A congratulatory address had previously been voted through in a public meeting. Appropriately, following Jewish custom recorded in the bible, debts were cancelled in the jubilee year. Debtors and criminals, to their delight, were released from prison, fifty-six prisoners altogether. They were regaled with a dinner, ale and a farewell present to the value of 10s in total (£42 today), paid for out of the surplus from the statue fund. Church bells rang in the morning and suitable sermons were preached to packed congregations eliciting generous contributions to charities. Many processions were formed, one to march through the streets to Great George Square to see the ceremony of the laying of the foundation stone of 'a statue to be erected by public subscription'. The front of the Town Hall was decorated with festoons of coloured lights round the columns and a brilliant display of fireworks concluded the celebrations in the evening.

Liverpool was devoted to King George III. Twenty years before, George's recovery from mental illness had been heralded by the ringing of bells and a twenty-one-gun

Above left: George III statue depicted on Herculaneum Pottery ware.

Above right: George III statue, 2009.

salute fired three times. A temporary roof over the central courtyard of the Exchange enclosed an area for a banquet, lit by 10,000 lights with chandeliers and crystal lamps 'forming the grandest spectacle of the kind, perhaps ever seen in this country'. A committee of the council greeted 800 guests at 7 o'clock, country dances began at nine, supper was announced at twelve and the company retired at 4 a.m. (double fares for the sedan chairmen!). Eight years later his granddaughter Charlotte died in childbirth, thus ending his hopes of a direct succession to the throne. A public meeting was held in the Town Hall to address a letter of condolence to his son, the Prince Regent. This was passed by a large majority in spite of some dissatisfaction with the prince. The equestrian bronze statue was not actually unveiled until 1822, two years after the king's death. This was partly due to a falling off in contributions after the initial enthusiasm and difficulties of settling on the right site. It was finally placed on the triangular piece of ground between London Road and Pembroke Place.

In the mid-eighteenth century pottery, and later porcelain, was a flourishing industry in Liverpool. The Herculaneum Pottery, which manufactured the plate illustrating the statue, was based in Toxteth from 1793 to 1841. It took workers from the potteries where Wedgwood made his 'Etruria' ware and adopted a superior Roman name. The Herculaneum Dock was later built on the site, now filled in for the City Quay residential development. Considering its bicentenary, the statue has survived to this day as shown in good condition.

Nelson Monument

Following Nelson's victory at Trafalgar in 1805, such was the warmth of feeling for him that the money needed for a memorial was raised within a little over two months. This compares with the ten years it took to raise only one third of the money that was needed for the statue of George III. But then, Nelson died heroically in action at sea and ensured that Liverpool merchants could once more ply their international trade unmolested. The freedom of the borough had been conferred on him in 1798 and in acknowledging the honour he wrote from the Victory 'I was taught the value of our West Indian possessions nor shall their interests be infringed while we have an arm to fight in their defence'. The statue was not finally unveiled until 1813, delayed by the processes of an open competition and the complexities of design and construction. A local architect was replaced by the famous Richard Westmacott from London. The total ensemble represents as much the rising maritime prowess of Liverpool as a commemoration of Nelson's death. Look below the cornice with the inscription 'ENGLAND EXPECTS EVERY MAN TO DO HIS DUTY'. Swags of laurel hang from behind lions' heads. Chains attached to rings in their mouths descend to four shackled prisoners in an attitude of dejection. They represent Nelson's four great naval victories at Cape St Vincent, the River Nile, Copenhagen and Trafalgar but may hint at slavery. Between the statues bronze bas-reliefs represent other naval actions in which Nelson fought. Above the cornice Nelson is depicted as an ideal nude figure with his amputated right arm covered by part of a flag. He stands with one foot on a cannon and the other

Nelson Monument.

on an enemy's corpse, holding upright a sword on which Victory is placing the last of four crowns. On Nelson's right, the figure of Death reaches out to claim him.

The monument was the first item of public sculpture to be erected in Liverpool. There are now some missing pieces and areas of corrosion to bear witness to its survival for 200 years over the forces of nature and pollution.

Necropolis

During the first part of the nineteenth century, most of the graveyards attached to the town churches of Liverpool were becoming overcrowded. The Necropolis Cemetery, opened in 1825, was one of the first privately financed burial grounds in the country. They were intended to be separate from religious establishments, places where civic worth could be commemorated without religious discrimination. The 5-acre site for individual graves was surrounded by an arcade containing family enclosures, fronted in masonry similar to the main entrance. This was appropriately grand and austere with resemblances to the Propylaea (the entrance to the Acropolis in Athens), which the architect John Foster Junior will have seen on his travels through Greece. Inside, accepted religious proprieties in tomb decoration were not slavishly observed, which ranged from an anchor to a child's crib. This was extremely successful with 18,000 burials in the first fifteen years, and the Necropolis became, together with St James' cemetery, two of the town's main tourist attractions, particularly for those of a melancholy nature.

Necropolis in 1844.

Because of overcrowding, it was closed to burials in 1898, and in 1913 the lodges, gates and walls were demolished. The following year it was reopened as Grant Gardens and survives as a park to this day on the corner of Everton Road and West Derby Road.

St James' Cemetery

By 1825 the quarry that had provided much of the sandstone for Liverpool's buildings was worked out. In spite of the recently opened Necropolis there was still a great need for another cemetery to relieve the lack of space in the town centre churches. It was decided to convert the quarry, and the architect John Foster Junior based his designs on the cemetery of Père-Lachaise in Paris. The Corporation gave the land and money for the cemetery to be connected to the Anglican Church. The completion in 1829 of a dramatic and romantic setting for graves in a cavernous arena was appropriately accompanied by

St James' cemetery.

one of the worst thunderstorms of the century. As can be seen, an ingenious system of carriageways for the funeral processions was carved out of the side of the escarpment. Catacombs cut into the rock face were enhanced by winding paths and trees below.

Many of the famous born in the Georgian era, and others, were laid to rest in the cemetery. Charles Wye Williams, inventor and one of the founders of the Peninsular and Oriental Company (P & O), lies alongside orphaned asylum children. By the time of the last interment in 1936, 57,774 people had been buried there. In the 1960s many of the interesting gravestones were removed to change the grounds to their present appearance.

George's Baths

George's Baths, completed in 1829 and designed by John Foster Junior, were named in honour of the reigning monarch, George IV. Confined, by their nature, to one storey, they were nevertheless clothed in classical garb. Even the chimney, incongruously short so as not to compete with St George's spire, was dignified with classical decoration. The interior featured innovative design and provision. The central reservoir of water was supplied by the river at high tide with a steam engine supplying the water for pumping, and there was a water filtration system. The ladies' quarters, with four hot and two cold private baths, were slightly smaller than the men's, which had the same number of rooms but cold, vapour and shower rooms as well. There were in addition large baths with sloping floors, dressing rooms and fireplaces. The print shows the baths viewed from the river. The masts of the ships in George's Dock can be seen behind.

The baths seem to have closed around 1907, sacrificed to the area's redevelopment associated with the filling in of George's Dock and the construction of the Mersey Dock and Harbour Board Building.

George's Baths, 1829, by Messrs Pynes.

Huskisson Mausoleum

William Huskisson entered the Liverpool scene in 1823 when he was President of the Board of Control. George Canning (later Prime Minister) had been one of the two Members of Parliament for Liverpool from 1812 to 1822. He nominated Huskisson for the office, who was duly elected without serious opposition. He was a popular representative for the town as he attended assiduously to the interests of the commercial community both nationally and locally, so much so that he was presented with a Service of Plate and then re-elected in 1826 (top of the poll) and again in 1828. He was appointed Colonial Secretary but angered the Duke of Wellington in Parliament. This was to prove fatal. When the railway cavalcade stopped at Rainhill on the opening of the Liverpool & Manchester Railway, he got out of his carriage onto the track to heal his quarrel with the duke, who was attending the national event as Prime Minister. Huskisson was mown down by the locomotive *Rocket* and died soon afterwards.

In the ensuing wave of sympathy £3,000 (£250,000 today) was raised to erect a memorial and the best Liverpool architect of the day, John Foster Junior, was commissioned to design it. John Junior had toured Greece during the Napoleonic Wars and, succeeding his father as Town Surveyor, had designed many public buildings in Liverpool since. In Athens, he had seen the monument of Lysicrates, erected in the fourth century BC by a sponsor to record his winning first prize at a dramatic festival. Huskisson's mausoleum is a delightful representation of this, particularly in the delicate acroteria (decorations on the edge of the roof) and the ornate Corinthian capitals at the top of the columns. It is set in St James's cemetery also designed by John Foster Junior, whose grave is only a few feet away from the mausoleum.

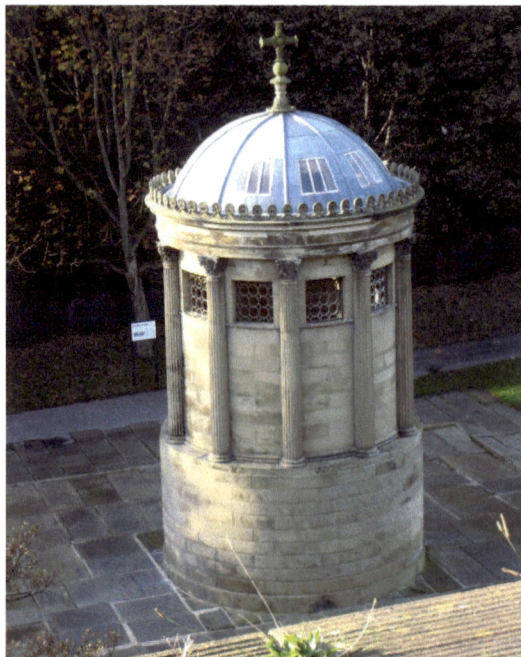

Huskisson Mausoleum.

3

CULTURE

Bluecoat School

The school was 'Dedicated to the promotion of Christian Charity and the training of poor boys in the principles of the Anglican Church in the year of Salvation 1717' (translation of the inscription in Latin over the entrance of the Blue Coat School

Bluecoat School. Observe the recalcitrant donkey. Is it symbolic?

for orphaned children). Another Latin inscription records how it was restored after being partly destroyed 'by the firebrands of the enemy'. It is the oldest building still standing in the centre of Liverpool and, at the time, the largest. Though Georgian in date, the building is actually a fine example of the Queen Anne style of architecture of the previous reign. Bryan Blundell funded it generously, but like so many Liverpool benefactors much of his money was derived from the slave trade or African Trade as it was called. Bryan was a sea captain and he, his son and grandson, and most of the trustees of the school, were involved in transatlantic shipping. He not only transported slaves from Africa to America but also servants and young children from Liverpool to be apprentices in the plantations. To start with, the fifty Bluecoat boarders spent two thirds of their time generating income for the school and a third in education. In addition, the merchants profited from the pupils who graduated to their apprenticeships. By the time of Bryan Blundell's death in 1756 the school housed fifty boys and thirty girls. His sons expanded the accommodation to educate 200 pupils.

In 1906 the school outgrew its premises and moved to a new building in Wavertree. Since then, it has functioned as an arts centre, now known simply as the Bluecoat.

St James's Walk

Liverpool's first park had been a quarry, was to become a cemetery and finish as a cathedral. Quarrying had started at least in the early eighteenth century and provided material for the phenomenal growth of the town, including the Town Hall, Corn Exchange and the churches of St Thomas, St Paul and St John. Stone was hauled out

St James's Walk in 1810.

through a tunnel to the top of Duke Street, which reverberated to the sound of carts trundling down to the town centre. The spoil was heaped up on the west side. In 1767 prices were high as a result of the severe winter and Thomas Johnson, the enterprising and compassionate mayor, devised a job creation scheme to level the mound and create a terrace 400 yards long. People promenaded admiring the extensive, beautiful and interesting view. Across a grassy green slope, the town was spread out in the foreground and, over the Mersey estuary, the Welsh mountains could be seen in the distance. A tavern or coffee house provided high-class dinners and entertainment. A shrubbery, managed by the Corporation, was open to the public every day but Sunday. On the other side of the quarry was a chalybeate spring, which attracted long queues hoping to be cured of rheumatism and many other ailments. The walk, otherwise known as Mount Zion or Mount Pleasant, took its name from St James' Church nearby. The Anglican Cathedral built on the site commands the same panorama but a vastly changed scene.

Archery Lodge

In the latter part of the eighteenth century, archery was a popular fashionable Liverpool pastime – for those who could afford it. Its adherents, called the Mersey Bowmen, considered it an 'old English' and 'manly' practice. They constructed a lodge where presumably equipment could be stored and associated social activities took place (the illustration appears to show a low-ceilinged ground floor with a grander well-lit room above). Over the upper window on the brick east front facing the street a carved stone

Archery Lodge in the eighteenth century.

represented a bow, arrows and a hunting horn. Each side was embellished with a stone tablet displaying the club's coat of arms: two arrows crossed with MB for Mersey Bowmen in appropriate old English letters. The adjacent 'shooting butts' were out in the countryside then, on Cazneau Street, now cut short by the approach road to the second Mersey Tunnel. The street has suffered a kaleidoscope of change from that day to this. By 1798 the club had broken up. Wings were added to the lodge, which became the dwelling and workshop of a cooper, which lasted until the 1850s. The nineteenth century saw the archery ground covered with housing, which lined the street along with a school and a fruit and vegetable market. That too has disappeared and the area is now an industrial estate with green open space on which archery could be practised once more!

Royal School for the Blind

Edward Rushton, born in Liverpool in 1756, was apprenticed aged eleven to a firm of West India merchants as a seaman. At the age of eighteen, he found himself aboard a ship transporting slaves and was accused by the captain of mutiny when he objected to the treatment of them. He caught ophthalmia from the slaves he was tending, became blind and founded the School for the Indigent Blind. It opened in two lodging houses in 1791, the first such school in Britain and the second to be founded in the world. In 1800 it moved into a purpose-built school, designed by John Foster Junior. Although there is a touch of classicism on the porch, it can be seen that the building precedes his visit to Greece, which initiated his elaborate Greek revival designs. It could accommodate seventy pupils, most of whom were from outside the town and lodged nearby. Much of

Royal School for the Blind before the extension.

the pupils' time was occupied in craft work but special attention was given to learning music so that they could qualify as organists or music teachers. Products that they made, such as baskets, sacks and shoes, were sold to generate income. However, many pupils were lodged in different houses near the school, and John Foster was asked to design a massive extension 'in a perfectly plain manner', which would provide residential accommodation for the pupils from outside the town. On completion in 1812, fifty-three males and eighteen females were admitted into the new building, which contained a refectory and dormitories for the pupils. There were rooms for music, work and storage, with a ropery and washhouses and baths in the cellar. A magnificent chapel also designed by John Foster was added later (see article under 'Churches').

The Prince of Wales (later George IV) bestowed royal patronage on visiting the school in 1806. It was demolished in 1852 to make way for an extension to Lime Street station. The replacement building on Hardman Street still survives but the school has moved to Wavertree.

Theatres

Drury Lane (Liverpool) was the site of a plain brick theatre built in 1759, about 81 feet in front by 48 feet deep, with boxes, pit and gallery, priced 3s, 2s and 1s, respectively. A typical programme performed by actors from the Theatre Royal in Drury Lane (London) started with Shakespeare's *Othello* at 7 o'clock (admittance was at 5). A 'new Scotch dance called the Highland Reel' enlivened the interval and the tragedy was alleviated afterwards by a pantomime *The Village Romps* and a farce *High Life Below Downstairs*. When did the performance finish?! A new theatre was built in Williamson Square in 1795 designed by Sir William Chambers, of international fame and practice. Thirty shareholders raised £6,000 at 5 per cent interest with a silver ticket entitling the bearer to every performance to any part of the house. The plain brick exterior was enhanced by a door frame in classical style, stone facings surrounding the windows and the royal coat of arms adorning the pediment. Inside, the stage was wider than that of Covent Garden at the time.

The popularity of the theatre can be gauged from riots which occurred in 1811 with considerable destruction of property (famine prices were rising and half-price admission was discontinued). Fledgling actors would make their name in Liverpool and return as celebrities from London or attract the gaze of nobility: Miss Farren became the Countess of Derby and Miss Mellon the Duchess of St Albans. The audience was lively and discriminating. The renowned Mrs Siddons was both mobbed with injuries to 'the body and dress' and compelled to leave the town. Clothes were torn from the backs of people struggling to obtain seats to see a popular young actor. Rival supporters of two actors who played the lead part disrupted a performance of Coriolanus. Not a syllable of speech could be heard and forms were thrown from the gallery into the pit. Fortunately, no one was injured on this occasion but on another, a woman was killed when a false alarm of 'fire!' was raised followed by a stampede to the exit down a narrow passage from the gallery. John Palmer gained fame and honour

Above: Theatre in Williamson Square as it appeared on opening in 1795.

Left: Rebuilt theatre of 1803.

when, after uttering the words 'There is another and a better world', he later collapsed and died on stage. On one occasion, some sailors dragged in a bull that had been baited at the village of West Derby, its entrance and exit facilitated by the shallow steps leading up from the pavement. However, a rapturous reception welcomed Paganini for a sequence of four concerts in 1832.

The theatre was completely rebuilt by John Foster Senior in 1803 with a grand semicircular façade 54 feet in height and 63 feet in width. A rustic base with neat classical doorcases was surmounted by pairs of Ionic pilasters (columns flat against the wall) enveloping windows with frames in classical style. Above them in bas relief were the royal coat of arms and emblems of comedy and tragedy. A decorated cornice runs round the top. The interior was reported to be spacious and elegantly decorated with good acoustics.

The theatre eventually suffered the indignity of being converted into a cold storage unit. The building was demolished for the construction of offices in the mid-1960s.

Athenaeum

The original Athenaeum building of 1797 was situated in Church Street. The coffee room (1,200 square feet) on the ground floor was furnished with London and provincial newspapers, trade lists, shipping lists, maps, charts and various periodical publications. The library above was for the use of subscribers or their nominees with an adjacent committee room and librarian's offices. It was lit by a skylight, which

Athenaeum of 1795.

was covered to prevent readers from being disturbed by the battering of the rain but which had the effect of diffusing a melancholy gloom, even at midday. The collection was enhanced by rare books, some belonging to William Roscoe, one of the founders. At the sale of his effects after his bankruptcy, his library was purchased by his friends, presented to him and then handed over by him to the Athenaeum. The 450 subscribers paid two guineas a year with the price of the shares rising from ten to twenty and then thirty guineas.

The building was demolished in 1929 to make way for road widening. The library of its successor in Church Alley has over 60,000 items described as 'one of the greatest proprietary libraries in the world'.

Royal Institution

In 1813 the banker Arthur Heywood chaired a meeting of leading residents of the town to establish an institution promoting 'the increase and diffusion of literature, science and the arts'. Shares to the total of £20,000 (over £1.6 million today) were raised. The premises of a merchant banker, Thomas Parr, built in around 1799, were purchased. The three-storey house faced Colquitt Street flanked by lower pavilion blocks: carriage house to the left, counting house to the right. A stone portico was added to enhance status and adaptations were made to accommodate a museum of natural history, chemical laboratory and lecture space to hold 500. It was incorporated by royal charter in 1822. Courses were delivered, meetings of literary societies were held and a historical gallery of art formed, mainly of pictures from William Roscoe's

Royal Institution by G. & C. Pyne.

collection. As with his books, when he became bankrupt, and they came up for sale, his friends bought them back and presented them to the institution. They include an incomparable group of early Italian and Flemish paintings now in the Walker Art Gallery.

Exhibition rooms held casts of Greek sculpture in which, in 1826, pictures of the American bird artist John James Audubon were displayed. He had sailed into Liverpool from the United States having failed to publish there his visionary work of the birds of North America depicted life size. Supported by William Roscoe and the Rathbones, his pictures were exhibited in the Royal Institution, drawing large crowds. Gaining connections and confidence in Liverpool, he went on to publish his books in London, the last one selling at auction for $9.65 million.

In 1900 Fanny Calder moved her Domestic Science College into the building where it stayed for most of the century until taken over by John Moores University. It now houses a restaurant, meeting place and active social hub.

Union Newsroom

It is an indication of the thriving intellectual life of the town at the time that within the space of five years (1797 to 1802) four cultural institutions were opened, three of them in new buildings: the Athenaeum, the Union Newsroom, and the Lyceum. Only the Royal Institution was adapted.

The Union Newsroom was opened on 1 January 1801, the day England was united with Ireland. The architect, John Foster Senior, had submitted plans for the Lyceum but, although approved by most of the committee, they were considered too costly. A dissident group who disagreed with the successful design chose John Foster's for the Union. The politics of the period is confused and may have played a part in the process.

Union Newsroom
in 1810.

The Lyceum was a Tory institution, and Foster was part of the Tory cabal that was in control at the time, but the Union was radical or Whig.

The choice of site was significant. At the time, mercantile operations were conducted near the houses of the merchants themselves and Duke Street was the aristocratic region of trade. The London morning papers reached Liverpool early the following morning, and the London evening papers the following evening. It suited the select circle living in the area to call in at the Union on their way to and from town. The arched windows of the newsroom were of simple Georgian design but elaborate arms of the Union adorned the roof. Inside, in a segment arch over the entrance to the bar, hung an allegorical painting by Fusili. England appeared at an altar receiving Scotland and Ireland into her embrace with figures representing the rivers Thames and Shannon. With 258 subscribers, the Union was smaller than the Lyceum. Its coffee room was only 46 feet by 49 feet, with two recesses of 17 square feet and 18 feet high. The library was of similar dimensions lit by a circular dome and constructed so as to diffuse an even light throughout.

Extensions were added in the same style and the interior has now been converted into offices.

Botanic Garden

The conservatory was the centrepiece and most important element of the Botanic Garden of 1800. The driving force behind fundraising was William Roscoe, lawyer, art collector and historian, and also a keen botanist who published a learned work on plants of the Ginger family. The conservatory provided ideal conditions for their

Botanic Garden in 1810.

cultivation as it was designed to create a year-round tropical humid climate provided by a steady bottom heat from fermenting bark. It was 240 feet in length with a maximum height of 24 feet, divided into five sections with different climatic regimes. There was also a large area where beds were planted with examples arranged on the principles of Linnaeus. Aquatic plants were displayed in a pond and a building housed a curator, herbarium and library. A rockery exhibited plants in their natural habitat. No fewer than 4,823 different species and cultivars were listed in their first plant catalogue. In his extensive address to those of the 300 proprietors who attended the inauguration, Roscoe spoke of the commercial and medicinal advantages to be gained from the scientific study and experimentation of imported fruit, grain and vegetables: 'Is it not probable that the improvement of plants by artificial means is yet in its infancy and may be carried to an indefinite degree of perfection?' Prescient indeed!

Unfortunately, the Botanic Garden was soon enveloped by the growing town, which spoilt the setting and exhaled pollution. The collection and membership were increasing so in 1836 the garden was moved to a more spacious site further out in Wavertree. Even mature trees were moved, a difficult operation with horses and carts. A new lodge was built, which has survived to this day, but the glasshouses were destroyed by a bomb in the Second World War.

Lyceum

An etching dedicated to the architect Thomas Harrison of Chester shows two faces of the Lyceum. Viewed from Church Street, the façade presents elegant central windows framed by imposing Ionic pilasters with superior pedimented windows on each side. The Bold Street front displays an imposing portico of Ionic columns and pediment of

Lyceum.

grander proportions, now cruelly overshadowed by buildings on the street. It led to the Liverpool Library and a newsroom. Opened in 1802, it takes its name from the school of Aristotle in ancient Athens, a city that, along with Rome, Liverpool later sought to emulate its culture and character.

The Liverpool Library, founded in 1758, was one of the oldest private subscription libraries in the country. It stemmed from a discussion group held in the house of William Everard, schoolteacher and mathematician, in St Paul's Square. A subscription to the *Monthly Review* and purchase of other books led to a collection in a chest in William's parlour, which was circulated among members of the group. The first catalogue listed 450 volumes with 109 subscribers. In 1787 the collection moved first into new purpose-built premises for an institution that boasted many prominent literati and then in 1802 into the Lyceum.

The Lyceum library contained over 10,000 volumes in various branches of literature, available for circulation among the 893 proprietors, the first circulating library in Europe. It also enabled merchants to meet and discuss the latest business developments. A coffee room, 68 feet long and 48 feet wide, was furnished with a large collection of London, provincial and foreign newspapers, and a variety of magazines, reviews and maps. Merchants could also view the all-important direction of the wind from the weathervane as they arrived and also inside from an indicator that it controlled in the newsroom!

By the 1970s the Lyceum had an air of blackened dilapidation and in the 1980s was threatened with demolition for shopping redevelopment but saved by a vigorous conservation campaign. In recent times, the interior has been converted for different uses, including a post office and restaurant.

Wellington Rooms

The Wellington Rooms, funded by public subscription, were opened in 1816 as a venue for the Wellington Club. A competition for the design was won by Thomas Aikin, a London architect, who moved to Liverpool to oversee the work and stayed to complete

Wellington Rooms in 2006.

other commissions. As originally built, the projecting portico entrance (on the left) was open but later it was filled in because it gave insufficient protection against wind and rain, so the columns are now disfigured by being converted into pilasters as seen. On the left was an open porch for sedan chairs and on the right another one for carriages but these have also been filled in. The decorative detail would appeal to those versed in the classics: the portico was based on the Monument of Lysicrates in Athens and the capitals of the columns on the Temple of Vesta at Tivoli with acroteria (ornamental decorations) at roof level. Inside, a vestibule and anteroom lead to cloakrooms, a supper room 50 by 25 feet with space for a small orchestra, a card room 44 by 25 feet and a ballroom 80 by 37 feet with plaster decoration.

For over thirty years after the war, the building was used as the Liverpool Irish Centre but now volunteers are clearing the foliage growing on it like an ancient ruin prior to refurbishment and redevelopment.

Mechanics Institute

A Mechanics School of Arts was established in 1825 with the aim of providing lectures and evening classes for adults whose education had been neglected. Different premises were used until the present building was opened in 1837. Unfortunately, because of over expectation of audience abilities and teaching of poor quality, numbers were not as great as anticipated. To remedy this, a lower school was started in 1835, which attracted pupils keen to lay the foundation of an education before they started work and an upper school for older students followed. The name was changed to the Liverpool Mechanics Institution in 1832, known later as the Liverpool Institute. The imposing façade displays the date the original school was established.

Mechanics Institute.

The school was closed in 1985. However, through the initiative and funding of Paul McCartney, a former student, it has been adapted for university level higher education, known as LIPA (Liverpool Institute of Performing Arts).

Aintree Racecourse

Liverpool horse racing was first established on marshland in nearby Crosby in 1774. Although the races there were not well supported, an associated ball or assembly at the Exchange attracted at least 350 people. However, a dreadful thunderstorm in 1781 that spoilt the amusements of the day contributed to its abandonment there in 1786. Aintree racecourse was opened in 1829 with a grandstand built for the first race. The first Grand National was run there in 1839. An imaginative painting depicts the beautiful grandstand built in 1829 by the Liverpool architect John Foster Junior. Graceful and decorative, it was designed in an elegant classical style and held 2,000 spectators. It incorporated vestibules on the ground floor and a huge refreshment room on the first floor (91 by 22 b y17 feet high) with fifteen windows, a balcony and withdrawing rooms. Unfortunately, it burnt down in 1892.

Besides archery, favourite sports of the upper class included tennis (with two courts at one time), cricket and, at various taverns, skittles and bowls. Other sports were not so genteel. Cockfighting was even encouraged by the Earl of Derby from his nearby stately home at Knowsley. Dog fighting was frequent and bullbaiting preceded the opening of the Queen's Dock. A bull was attacked by dogs to prove their courage at the West Derby village annual wakes and then led in triumph into the town.

Aintree Racecourse grandstand.

4
HEALTH

Old Infirmary

In 1745, the year of the Jacobite rebellion, plans were made to raise money for the Old Infirmary. The rebellion and its aftermath delayed its opening until 1749. Liverpool remained firmly loyal to the Royalist cause and raised a regiment, the 'Liverpool Blues', to fight for the king. It was in action in Warrington against the rebels and distinguished itself in relieving the siege of Carlisle. It was then disbanded but Liverpool was later troubled by anti-Catholic riots.

Next to the Infirmary was the old Lunatic Asylum and the Seamen's Hospital of 1752, an almshouse for 'decayed seamen, their widows and children'. Individual subscriptions covered the cost of the building and the Corporation donated a field with a lease of 999 years. In 1807 the infirmary (combined with the old Lunatic Asylum) was in fine

Old Infirmary in 1810 and the Haymarket.

financial fettle. The income was derived largely from subscriptions of the wealthy, public collections, dividends from investments and receipts from services rendered. Expenses were mostly incurred in food, maintenance of the building and salaries of the domestic staff (but not of the medical staff). Enough profit was made on the day-to-day running of the establishment to make substantial further investment. Of the 1,245 inpatients treated during that year, 702 were cured and only thirty-seven died; of 685 outpatients, 438 were cured and only seventeen died. Pupils were charged a small amount for their practical training, which gave them experience in prescriptions and operations. The old Lunatic Asylum nearby, run in conjunction with the Infirmary, treated 118 patients in the same year (1807), of which forty-six were cured. The infirmary, in the Haymarket area, was replaced by a new one in Brownlow Hill in 1825.

Workhouse or House of Industry

In 1723, the overseers of the parish of Liverpool agreed to take thirty-six houses for the reception of the parish poor. They had been built by Alderman Bryan Blundell on the south side of the Blue Coat School, which he had funded a few years before. A later building fit for the purpose proved inadequate for the growing numbers of the indigent poor and a much larger poor house was completed in 1771 at the top of Brownlow Hill. The centre of the building, designed in typical Georgian symmetrical style, was dignified by a pediment above the main entrance and a decorative cupola on the roof. The accommodation included a committee room and apartments for the overseers and supervisory staff. There was a large common dining hall and working space on two storeys for useful tasks such as spinning, picking cotton and oakum, and weaving linen and bed sacking. In July 1806, out of the 947 poor in the house, sixty-nine were aged under two years and 225 aged two to ten. There were very few teenagers. Successive decades averaged about 100 until the age of seventy.

The Workhouse was demolished in 1931 and the site is now occupied by the Catholic Cathedral.

Workhouse or House of Industry in 1844.

Dispensary in 1810.

Dispensary

The Dispensary was the first design of a public building by John Foster Senior, who, eight years later, became the Corporation Surveyor. As can be seen, it was very much in the traditional Georgian mould with the façade adorned by a pediment in a simple classical style. The ground floor windows are typical Georgian with a fan arch above the rectangular base. Unusually, the portico is curved and there was a small figure of the Good Samaritan above it with balancing decorations on each side. The plaque was well executed by John Deare, a Liverpool born sculptor who later went on to a successful career in Rome but died there tragically, and young.

When opened in 1778 the parish poor were being attended by just one apothecary on an annual salary who was unable to cope with the growing numbers. A society was formed, committed to paying a subscription to fund the institution which was added to a contribution from the parish. Six physicians and three surgeons were employed to provide prescriptions on a rota basis at the dispensary or at the patients' homes. In the following two years, the children of the Blue Coat Hospital and the prisoners of the Borough Gaol were brought into the care system with payment of an annual sum. Physicians and surgeons also attended the Seamen's Hospital, the Almshouses, the Workhouse, the House of Correction, the Fever Recovery Hospital, the Low Hill Workhouse and the Lunatic Asylum. By 1807 the number of patients treated per year amounted to over 12,000.

The building was sold in 1829 and demolished for redevelopment. Its work was then divided between two dispensaries. One, in the south in Upper Parliament Street, was a house conversion; the other, in the north in Vauxhall Road, moved into new purpose-built premises in 1831.

Fever Recovery Hospital

The Fever Recovery Hospital, otherwise known as the Fever Ward or House of Recovery, was adjacent to the Workhouse which supplied it with the necessary provisions. An apothecary and matron, resident on the ground floor, were salaried

Fever Recovery Hospital
in 1810.

but six dispensing physicians gave their services free in rotation to look after the patients. The infectious diseases included typhus, scarlet fever, smallpox, measles and whooping cough. Although the accommodation was rather cramped, the upper storeys were subdivided into different wards to prevent infection. Unfortunately, people who would benefit from treatment did not realise the quality of care that they would receive and were reluctant to attend. Physicians also failed to analyse data and link with the community to anticipate and prevent infection. However, it admitted 517 patients in the first year of opening in 1806.

New Infirmary

Behind the impressive 204-feet façade of the infirmary, much thought had been given to patients' welfare. The wings were set back 82 feet without any recesses to allow

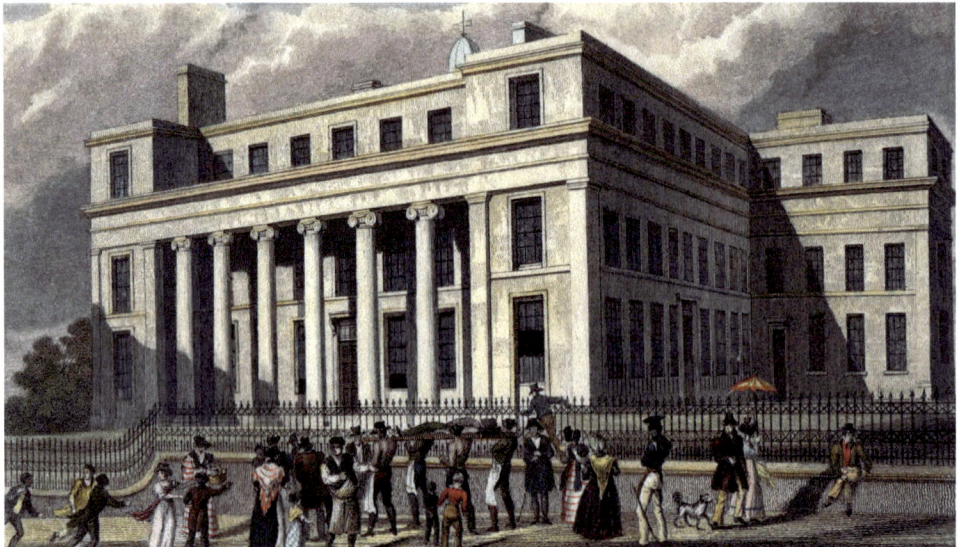

New Infirmary.

maximum access of light and air. Heating and ventilation were installed of the latest design following the system of Charles Sylvester. The well-lit wards with high ceilings and 138 windows of larger than usual height occupied the top two storeys (although this gave a top heavy look). The ground floor was reserved for administration with twenty committee rooms and offices, and a ward for emergencies. The basement served for 'domestic utility': the kitchens were particularly praised for their compactness and their use of fire and steam for cooking with 'scarcely a burning ember' to be seen. John Foster Junior orchestrated the imposing appearance in true Georgian style. Six giant Ionic columns the height of two storeys supported the portico in front with another six pilasters of the same order in the angles.

It was replaced in 1890 on the same site by the Royal Infirmary designed by Alfred Waterhouse. Now converted to other uses, that has been superseded by the Royal Liverpool University Hospital.

New Lunatic Asylum

The old Lunatic Asylum had been opened in 1749 in the Haymarket area at the same time as the old Infirmary and alongside it. In 1829 a new Lunatic Asylum was opened to join the New Infirmary on Brownlow Hill. Like the infirmary, two wings projected forwards to admit light and air for health of body and mind. Measuring 161 feet wide and 150 feet in depth, it was surrounded by an open space for exercise enclosed by a high brick wall. The wings comprised wards with cells on each side and the centre had mainly day rooms, spacious and well lit, the largest of which was 25 feet by 19 feet. There was similar accommodation on the first floor with warm baths and keepers' rooms. The building was heated and ventilated by the Sylvester system, like the Infirmary. The basement included kitchens, cellars and storerooms. There was room for sixty patients with some superior 'private' accommodation. It was simple and appropriately restrained in appearance compared with the infirmary, although designed by the same architect. As can be seen, rustication (large rough blocks of stone) stretched up to the windowsills on the first floor with minimum dentil decoration in the cornices above.

New Lunatic Asylum.

5
CHURCHES

St Peter's Church

The church was consecrated in 1704 just before the Georgian era began. It is typical of so many later churches with an octagonal tower but this one was distinguished by pinnacles on each corner representing a candlestick and a gilt vane resembling a flame. Inside was a gallery for the children of the nearby Blue Coat Hospital. On the south side of the chancel was a costly monument of marble erected in 1858 to the memory of Foster Cunliffe. A portrait of him was also displayed together with a vase, supposed to contain his heart, with orphans depicted one on each side lamenting the death of their benefactor. It is an example of the hidden shameful background to the Georgian

St Peter's Church.

history of Liverpool: slavery. Foster Cunliffe is extolled, in the fulsome language customary at the time, for his sagacity, honesty and diligence in procuring wealth for himself and his country (he was said to be one of the wealthiest in the land). In fact, he, his two brothers, his father and his son made huge profits for themselves through slave trading. His grandson, Sir Foster Cunliffe, when writing his family's genealogy, made no reference to their involvement.

In 1880 St Peter's became the pro-cathedral of Liverpool until it was demolished in 1922. A bronze Maltese cross in Church Street marks the place where the altar stood.

St George's Church

The architect of St George's was Thomas Steers, who also designed the Old Dock. Consecrated in 1734, it was constructed on the site of the demolished castle. Although the church, following good biblical principles, was founded on rock, the spire, inexplicably and unfortunately, was built on the remains of the moat. A huge crack

St George's with arcade in 1810.

St George's Church tower in the eighteenth century.

from top to bottom appeared as a result of settlement and in 1809 John Foster Senior, Corporation Surveyor, ordered the spire to be demolished. The rebuild was designed by his son, John Foster Junior. The lofty spire was visible from all over the town, from a distance by land from Everton and over water by sea from Tranmere.

The four tiers of its supporting tower are a perfect introduction to the four orders (or styles) of Greco-Roman architecture: Doric, Ionic, Corinthian and Composite. If you designed a building with one tier on top of another, it was customary to place them in that order starting from the bottom. Only rarely are all four represented in this way as here. The sturdiest, as measured by the ratio of height to width, is the Doric, which is also the plainest with no embellishment round its base and a simple ringed decoration at the top (capital) of the column. The slenderer Ionic columns are distinguished by the scrolls adorning its capital and a decorative base. The Corinthian is more decorative still with acanthus leaves on its capitals while the Composite, as the name implies, is a combination of Ionic and Corinthian. All these may be spotted on the detail of an etching of the tower. In between the pilasters (flattened columns) of the top octagonal tier figures of saints have been painted. Along the nave, the rounded windows with keystones were separated by pilasters, double at each end. The Doric order in which these were styled was continued in the frieze above with alternate triglyphs (grooved decorations) and metopes (flat panels). Decorative urns completed the decoration at roof level.

The church was surrounded by a fruit and vegetable market, with produce coming readily from overseas. The arcade of six arches at ground level provided shade and shelter for marketeers and customers. The two delightful octagonal pavilions housed the services of the clerk of the market at one end and at the other a watchman with lock-up prison and fire bell above. Underneath was a vault for the internment of distinguished families. The church was built by the Corporation and used as a chapel by their members. The mayor, council and aldermen occupied seats rented by the Corporation for their use. John Newton, former slave owner, later abolitionist, after leaving the sea and becoming a surveyor, preached in the church. However, an aggressive sermon was preached in 1863 against the appointment of a Jewish mayor. Its resulting abandonment by the Corporation led to the flourishing church's decline, closure and demolition in 1897. The Victoria Monument now stands on the site.

St Nicholas' Church

The original building of about 1360 was the only place of worship in the town and a chapel of ease (for those who did not find it easy to attend the parish church at Walton). In 1699 a separate parish was formed jointly with St Peter's. The nave, together with aisles added in the seventeenth century, was replaced in 1744 by an ornate Gothic structure. An engraving shows how the gabled building in front (the old Tavern) had formed part of the original church. Soon after, the churchyard was extended to include some land reclaimed from the river, which came right up to the boundary wall of the church. A spire was added to the old tower but this caused the added weight and the

Left: St Nicholas'
towards the end
of the eighteenth
century.

Below:
St Nicholas' in
1844.

vibrations of the bells precipitated a sudden collapse of the tower in 1810. It fell onto, and through, the roof of the nave just as the bells had ceased ringing for a Sunday morning service. Twenty-five people, including seventeen girls from the Moorfields Charity School, were killed. In 1815 an imposing new tower was built in an extremely decorative Gothic style. As pictured in a watercolour of 1844, it became the tallest building in Liverpool until surpassed In 1868 by the Welsh Presbyterian Church in

Toxteth. In 1940 an incendiary bomb destroyed all the church except for the tower, which has survived to this day.

A 1773 guidebook recorded two memorials of note. One, representing Grief, was in memory of Elizabeth Clayton, wife of William Clayton, who died 'in the 78th year of her age 1745'. The other monument recorded that William had died in 1715 'being a great incourager of trade and having good judgement in it represented the borough in six distinct parliaments'. In fact, he had made his fortune as a slave trader and dealer in slave-grown goods. When their daughter Sarah took over the family fortune, she most successfully used it to develop lucrative coal mining interests. She was instrumental in the design of the new exchange building and founded Clayton Square, demolished in 1989, whose replacement still bears her name.

St Thomas' Church

Between 1750, when it was built, and 1822, when its spire was demolished 'to prevent mischief', St Thomas' was visible and recognisable in any view of Liverpool. Its elegant tall spire (216 feet) stood out from its crowding neighbours in the heart of the town near the Old Dock. It was half the height of the steeple as a whole but its height caused

St Thomas' in 1810.

endless trouble. In 1757 a hurricane blew down 42 feet of its height. The rebuild was 18 feet shorter but even so it was struck by lightning and suffered storm damage. It became so unstable and rocked so much when buffeted by high winds that it could be seen to vibrate from a quarter of a mile away. As can be seen in the engraving, there were two rows of windows interspersed by double pilasters in the Ionic order, which continue in the decoration of the second tier of the tower. The Corinthian tier above it is topped by incongruous Gothic pinnacles. The architect Henry Sephton made sure he displayed all his expertise: unusually, the chancel consists of a half octagon extension jutting out at the east end (on the right) with an overhung Venetian window. The interior was well lit and paved. Although the paving, provision of pews and Corinthian decoration were praised, two conspicuous gilt figures on each side of the organ were condemned in a guidebook of the time as being 'the offspring of a puerile judgement and a barbarous taste'. The church was demolished in 1905.

St Paul's Church

St Paul's Square was laid out soon after 1760 in what had been from the early part of the century the aristocratic north end of the town. Mansions had been constructed there in a very pleasant and salubrious area around Old Hall Street, one of the seven ancient streets of the town. From it, fashionable folk could stroll down to 'Ladies' Walk', which stretched along the 'north shore' of the river. There they could promenade, enjoying the view across the river to the Welsh mountains beyond. Before the advent of the canal in the 1770s, a companion 'Maiden's Green' for courting couples extended inland. There was another 'Ladies Walk' along the line of what is now Duke Street with four lines of trees.

St Paul's as depicted on a Herculaneum Pottery plate.

St Paul's Church was completed in the square in 1769. It was designed in an imposing style, as befitted its neighbourhood, and financed by the Corporation. On three sides, steps led up to entrances framed by an imposing pediment held up by Ionic columns with urns on the balustrades above. It resembles its namesake in London with a dome and cupola. Inside, unfortunately, voices were lost in the dome and, although parchment was stretched across to improve the acoustics, the effect was unsightly. There were free seats for the poor on the floor of the nave for those who could not afford the gallery.

St Paul's was demolished in 1932 to make way for the Liverpool Boxing Stadium, itself demolished in 1987, and the site is now used as a car park.

St James' Church

St James' is unique in Liverpool as the oldest Anglican church in the city centre, and the only one from the Georgian period to have survived the ravages of time, war and the developers. And it is still worshipping today, virtually intact. Cuthbert Bisbrowne built the church as the centrepiece of a new town to be developed on the outskirts of Liverpool on land owned by the Earl of Sefton, who gave the site for the building of the church. The estate was to be called 'Harrington' in honour of the family name of the Earl's wife. Plots were to be sold for superior housing and the church was opened in 1775. Pews were sold (limited to residents of the parishes of Liverpool and Walton-on-the-Hill) which, with subsequent rents, generated income for the church. The interior was the usual arrangement for Georgian churches of a balcony on three

St James in the City.

sides. However, what was most unusual, if not unprecedented, was the use of cast-iron columns to support the galleries. These were among the prototypes in the land and led to a revolution in architectural possibilities throughout the world. Elegant and unobtrusive, as can be seen in the photo, they are slender with capitals decorated in classical style. More importantly, they have maintained their function steadfastly to this day. Another most unusual, if not unique, feature was an upper balcony at the west end in which the churchwardens had to do duty quelling the 'exuberance' of the children there. Bisbrowne's scheme, however, did not prosper as the building plots remained unsold, maybe because of the slump in trade caused by the American War of Independence and the actions of privateers. He was declared bankrupt in 1776.

The church was in the countryside and commanded a beautiful view across the river to the Welsh hills. The graveyard was often chosen as an attractive place for burials in preference to crowded town centre cemeteries. Sir John Gladstone (father of William Ewart, Prime Minister) chose it for the internment of his first wife. Eventually, the cemetery was crowded with 9,000 burials but was grassed over in 1901. The inscriptions on the tombstones were recorded and give an insight to personages of the time and their lives, for example Samuel Athill, who died aged twenty-nine in 1822. He 'had from his integrity and amenity of disposition, acquired the confidence and esteem of all who knew him. A severe and lingering illness, which he bore with exemplary patience and fortitude, caused his visit to this country, where it pleased God to remove him from a state of suffering, he died reposing his hopes on the mercy of

Above left: St James' iron columns supporting the gallery.

Above right: St James' monument of Jacob Aemelius Irving.

his redeemer'. In fact he was a plantation and slave owner, and the son of a plantation owner, and amazingly a 'free negro' of Antigua. The mother of his four children (he never married) was an enslaved woman. The diversity of church membership and Liverpool as a whole during the later Georgian period is shown by the records of the church and its monuments. Over a hundred black people were baptised there in the two decades from 1785 to 1805 hailing from all over the shores of the Atlantic and beyond. Many of them were mature adult baptisms.

In addition, there is a galaxy of twenty monuments, eighteen from the Georgian period, one of them for Edward Grayson, a shipbuilder. Several of his ships were used in the sugar trade, so indirectly he profited from the slave trade. His monument pays tribute to him as 'an honest man, an attractive relative and a sincere friend whose zeal in the defence of insulted innocence caused him to fall a sacrifice to the laws of false honour whereby the injured are unhappily compelled to expose themselves to destruction at the call of the aggressor'. At a trial after his death in 1804 it was revealed that a relative of his had been engaged to be married to William Sparling. However, William had called off the marriage and Edward, incensed, referred to William as a 'villain'. When word of this reached him, William demanded an apology from Edward, which was not forthcoming. A duel was arranged to be settled by pistols at dawn in Dingle Glen. Edward was killed. William and his second were put on trial for murder but acquitted.

Another monument was set up 'To the memory of Captain George Pemberton, Commander of the ship "Wilding" of Liverpool. Who died on the 20th day of November 1795 of the wounds he received in a most gallant action with a French privateer of superior force, when bound on a voyage to Jamaica. In which Captain Pemberton did honour to the character of a British Sailor, by destroying the enemy's ship and preserving his own'. Privateers were licensed pirates who affected Liverpool's fortunes greatly on both sides in the Napoleonic wars. This, the earliest monument, was put up by his employer, Moses Benson, who was a well-known wealthy Liverpool merchant and slave trader. The monument that is pictured was created by the widow of 'Jacob Aemelius Irving Esquire of Ironshore in the Island of Jamaica who died in 1812. Exemplary in all the relations of life, mild and gentle in disposition and manners, full of truth, honour and integrity, he acquired the love of all who knew him'. Ironshore was a sugar plantation with a strong family management over several generations.

The church went through various vicissitudes before it was condemned for demolition to make way for the construction of a ring road in 1972. Fortunately for St James', this was never built, and it survived to be adopted by the Churches Conservation Trust in 1976. It then remained in an increasingly derelict state until it was restored to the Church of England, reconsecrated in 2009 and revitalised by Revd Neil Short as St James in the City.

St Peter's Catholic Church

From the early 1800s Liverpool acted as a staging post for Irish migrants on their way to North America and many stayed. During the period 1821–31, Liverpool's population increased 38 per cent, the highest of any recorded decade. In the next

St Peter's Catholic Church, now 'Alma de Cuba'.

decade, the Irish population accounted for as much as 15 per cent of the total even before the refugees arrived fleeing from the great famine. There were, however, only four Catholic churches. The largest of these was St Peter's in Seel Street, opened in 1788. It was a simple unobtrusive, unadorned brick box with a gabled roof. The porch seen now was added in 1818. Full Catholic emancipation had yet to be enacted and, in 1745, during the Jacobite rebellion, a mob had burnt down St Edmund's Catholic Chapel, dating from 1736. St Patrick's in Park Place was opened in 1824. The poverty of the Irish population (and others) was alleviated most notably by Kitty Wilkinson, an immigrant from Londonderry, who was the only person around her to own a boiler in the cholera epidemic of 1832. She invited anyone to use it and soon after opened the first public washhouse in Liverpool.

The church ceased to be Catholic in 1976, acted as a Polish church for two years and was deconsecrated in 1993. It is now (from 2005) a bar and restaurant 'Alma de Cuba'.

Christ Church

John Houghton, Esquire, to whom the engraving is dedicated, was most generous in his provision for the church on Hunter Street. John was a distiller of the Bull Inn, in nearby Trueman Street, and paid for the whole of the church. He further endowed it with a good salary for the minister with further allowances for an organist, clerk and sexton. The 400

Christ Church from the
north, 1810.

free seats for the poor were rather cramped and too close to the roof in an upper gallery, which, with a lower gallery, stretched round three sides. There was a unique arrangement at the south (chancel) end. The organ pipes were divided into two, with a special gallery, which admitted light from the large window while the organist faced the congregation unseen. A splendid view could be obtained from the cupola, which lit the church and was accessed through the upper gallery. An even better view was given by climbing a ladder (quite safely) to a circular gallery nearly at the top.

The windmill as shown may not be merely for decoration as Hunter Street is on rising ground and a watercolour of the time shows three windmills on nearby Copperas Hill. The church was consecrated in 1800 but John did not enjoy his church for long as he died in 1809. However, it survived until demolition in 1920.

St Michael's, Pitt Street

One of the most showy churches in Liverpool, St Michael's had a superb setting as the focal point of an expansive square that also included a graveyard. John Foster Junior (Senior's son) had just come back from a 'grand' tour from Greece in 1812. His father would have sent him on the usual grand tour of Italy to refine his talent for architecture, but this proved impossible as Napoleon had control of Italy at the time. John Junior pioneered the Greek Revival style in Liverpool that predominated in public buildings for the next thirty years. Construction of St Michael's, his first design, started in 1816 on an ambitious scale. The tower and steeple, 203 feet high, were modelled on St Martin in the Fields in London. Foster aimed to show off his expertise in the classical style through the intricate detail of the four tiers of the tower. The west end (to the left) sported an unnecessarily extended portico and the east end (to the right) an unusual inset portico, purely for decoration. Seven years later, construction had still not been finished and the project had cost £35,000 (£4.3 million today). An

St Michael's from the south-east, 1844.

Act of Parliament was passed to make over the patronage to the Corporation, who contributed the equivalent of another £1.3 million (today) to secure its completion after yet another three years.

The body of this beautiful church fourteen years in the making was destroyed in one night by the Blitz. The spire was left standing disconsolately alone but had to be demolished as well soon afterwards.

St George's Church, Everton

Two landmark Liverpool firsts were posted by St George's Church in Everton. In its construction, the Liverpool iron founder Thomas Cragg was the first in the world to use prefabricated cast-iron sections, and in its architecture Thomas Rickman pioneered the Perpendicular style in England (this was a term that Rickman used in the authoritative

St George's Everton interior.

book he published in 1817 in which he defined the different styles of English medieval ecclesiastical architecture). First, Cragg's cast-iron skeleton frame was faced in sandstone with castellations at roof level. Then, outside, Rickman exploited the possibilities of cast iron to add pinnacles to the buttresses (now removed) and create large windows with cast-iron tracery to admit extra light. Inside, the ceiling was decorated in a similar delicate style and galleries supported by slender cast-iron columns afforded a freer view for the congregation, a device that had been pioneered in St James' Church in 1774.

Rickman collaborated again with Cragg to manufacture St Michael in the Hamlet, as the name indicates in a village near Liverpool, which was appropriately designed to resemble a medieval Cheshire country church. Both these churches survive, but a third Cragg church, St Philip's on Hardman Street was demolished in 1882.

Chapel of the School for the Blind

A chapel for the School for the Indigent Blind was started in 1818, designed by John Foster Junior. Its most striking exterior feature was the portico in Doric style, almost an exact copy of the Temple of Aphaea on the island of Aegina, which John Junior had visited in Greece. As can be seen, the interior was especially beautiful with columns in the Ionic order. Apart from being an extension to the religious education of the pupils, the chapel encouraged the pupils to perfect their musical skills. It was a pity they could not appreciate its aesthetic beauty, which attracted visitors to come and listen to their performances. Capable of holding a thousand people (half of them the public) it was, in the absence of a cathedral, the fashionable church of the town. The music

Chapel of the School for the Blind interior.

was recommended in a guidebook as 'well worthy of a visit, the service being most admirably chaunted, as in our cathedrals'. The chaplain had a reputation for preaching and, in fact, did so for nearly fifty years. It was in what was a prosperous area at the time and was supported by many eminent Liverpool citizens. Outsiders were expected to put silver coin into a plate as they entered.

Subsequently, the chapel had an interesting history. In 1851, it was moved bodily to a new site opposite the Philharmonic Hall to make way for extensions to Lime Street station. It served alongside the new school that had been built there until it was demolished in 1931 when the school was enlarged. Some of the columns were dumped at Camp Hill in Wavertree but one was set up as a memorial to the architect near his grave in St James' cemetery (through the trees to the right of the photo on page 33).

St Andrew's Presbyterian Church

St Andrew's Church in Rodney Street is the finest surviving example of the Greek Revival architecture of John Foster Junior. The main body of the church is brick with stucco but John Foster designed a beautiful stone façade with an Ionic portico, balustrade and corner towers topped by aedicules (in the form of mini temples) and

St Andrew's Presbyterian Church.

delicate cupolas to crown them. The Scottish Presbyterian community at the time was thriving, nearly doubling in the three years from 1835 to a total of 5,704. Skilled and professional Scots had become an increasingly powerful force in the latter part of the eighteenth century. John Gladstone, father of the future prime minister, was one of the leading Scottish Presbyterian merchants who asserted their rights to be represented on the Council which discriminated against dissenters. Their solidarity was expressed in the construction of six chapels by 1831, one of them a most ornate and well-furnished chapel in Paradise Street. A dispute over the appointment of a minister of another chapel in Oldham Street led to the breakaway congregation here in Rodney Street in 1823.

The building was badly burned in 1983 and lost its tower on the left. This has been rebuilt and the body converted to accommodation for John Moores University students.

St David's Church

Attendance at chapel was an important part of Welsh identity and in 1831 six chapels served the community in the heart of the town. The Calvinistic Methodists were particularly well represented but there was also provision for Wesleyan Methodists and Independents. The Industrial Revolution attracted, or forced, Welsh people to the nearest large town bringing with them the need for extra housing. Slate, brick, stone and timber from Wales for housing accompanied Welsh managers and workers ready to profit from engagement in the building trade. By 1813 one in ten persons living in Liverpool was of Welsh origin, more than any other immigrant group in Britain.

St David's Church on Brownlow Hill.

In 1826 St David's Church or the Welsh Church was opened on the north side of Brownlow Hill on the site of Ranelagh Gardens. For once, the architect John Foster did not show off his classical credentials. Sensitively, he designed an unpretentious exterior, which must have inspired immediate affection for the simplicity and honesty of the minimal and appropriate decoration outside that reflected the worship within. The services preserved the Welsh language and, by encouraging English, helped the process of integration.

The church was demolished in 1910 to make way for extensions to the Adelphi Hotel.

Oratory

The Oratory was created by John Foster Junior as a chapel for St James' cemetery. Unlike the marble Parthenon, its brick core was faced with grey gritstone but it was a perfect Greek temple of the same Doric order as the Parthenon. Above the columns is the typical Doric pattern of grooved triglyphs alternating with metopes or panels. The roof is decorated with acroteria that stand out against the sky. The Parthenon is completely surrounded by columns but smaller versions were often 'hexastyle' with six columns only on each end, as here. It was lit by skylights in the roof. Inside, many of the monuments date from the Georgian era and are sculpted in classical form, four of them by Sir Francis Chantrey, the most popular and successful of nineteenth-century British sculptors. One of the statues commemorates William Ewart (1763–1823), son of a Scottish minister, who settled in Liverpool and became a prosperous merchant. William Ewart Gladstone, four times Prime Minister, took his first names from him as William Ewart was a close friend of his father, John Gladstone. Both made great profits

Above left: The Oratory, an Acropolis and Parthenon in miniature.

Above right: The statue of William Ewart in the Oratory.

from slavery: William from trading and John from plantations. The marble statue of William Ewart was completed in 1833, making it one of the originals in the Oratory. It shows him, not in classical form or pose, but in contemporary dress seated cross legged in an armchair. He is holding a paper from which he appears to be expounding to his audience. The Oratory also contains an epitaph to the architect: 'On his return from long and arduous travels in the pursuit of his art, he enriched his native town with the fruits of his genius, industry and integrity'.

St Luke's Church

The tower of St Luke's Church stands high at the top of Bold Street, its commanding position enhanced by a flight of steps up to the west door. John Foster Senior drew up the original designs in 1802 and the foundation stone was laid by the mayor in 1811, but it was not consecrated until 1831. The land had been given specifically, as so often by the Earl of Derby, and it is difficult to imagine that the long delay in completion may have been caused by a land dispute. By 1831 John Foster Junior had taken over from his father and made alterations to the original design. Neither of the Fosters had a penchant for Gothic architecture and John Junior led the Greek Revival style in Liverpool. An extended choir was unusual (based on the Beauchamp Chapel in Warwick). It may be that Thomas Rickman who was living in Liverpool at the time had an influence on its Gothic design, which he would have identified as perpendicular. Notably, a large number of male and female heads cover the building. Eight bells were hung but unfortunately a peal of 5,056 changes lasting three hours and two minutes

St Luke's Church from the west.

was too overpowering for the neighbourhood. Complaints were made that the value of houses was being affected and it was even suggested that the bells should be transferred to St Martin's Church (which would have caused complaints there).

The interior of the church was completely destroyed by enemy bombing in 1941. For a time the church was neglected and in danger of demolition but it has now been restored as a memorial of the war.

Scotland Road

As the name implies, Scotland Road was the road leading out of Liverpool towards the north. At the same time as Georgian architecture thrived on a grand scale on the other side of the city, the land to the north along Scotland Road was sprouting much smaller terraces. The streets did, however, rejoice in great sounding names of England's naval heroes, Nelson and Collingwood, the statesman Grenville and poets Homer, Virgil and Dryden. There the development stopped in 1830 with open fields beyond. This point was marked by a Roman Catholic chapel of St Anthony first erected around 1806 and French prisoners of war would have attended the church under supervision from the prison in Great Howard Street. It was replaced by the present Gothic 'early pointed period' church in 1833, still there today. It can be spotted in the very far distance of the illustration.

Subsequently, the nearer, Scottish, church St Peter's was opened in 1843. On the other side of the street this way is a small Methodist chapel that opened in 1843. These churches demonstrate the variety of religious beliefs in the area and Liverpool as a whole.

Scotland Road. Notice the street pump in the centre.

6
ARCHITECTURE

Rodney Street

The balance of a grand Georgian terrace is beautifully illustrated by this view of Rodney Street (named after the admiral who distinguished himself in the American War of Independence). Designed to look like a Renaissance palace (a good selling point for Georgians!), the centre point is a five-bay house (far left of the picture) distinguished from the others by an overall pediment and breaking forward into the street. On each side (the far one out of view) are six houses, each of three bays only, the first four with paired doorways and the end ones with a single doorway. They jut forward in importance to match the house at the centre. The doorways, flanked by attached Doric columns, have rounded fanlights and pediments to reflect the overall scheme for the terrace. All the windows have wedge-shaped lintels and are sashed,

Rodney Street.

some with glazing bars and iron balconies, and some blind. There was no scheme for the street as a whole but all the houses were of brick and most of three bays. It was laid out by William Roscoe and others in 1783–84 when prosperity and confidence returned at the end of the war and attracted the wealthy with its peace and quiet away from the town centre. John Gladstone lived opposite at No. 62 where William, future Prime Minister, was born. Like Harley Street in London architecturally, it was also the home of doctors.

Castle Street

At the beginning of the Georgian era, Castle Street ran from the second town hall at one end to the decaying castle at the other. The Corporation negotiated with the Earl of Derby for the castle and its land and in 1734 St George's Church was built on the site of the castle. A new town hall was built in 1747 but the west side of Castle Street was covered by a dense and confused mass of buildings stretching down to the river. The view of Castle Street in 1786 looks north towards the Town Hall/ Exchange before the fire of 1795. There is ample material here both on the building sites and in the streets for those researching health and safety! The buildings on the left, west, side are being demolished and a new Heywood's Bank has reached roof level. This was supplemented by another one illustrated later in this book. The widening of the street had the effect of opening up the view of the Town Hall from this point and, later on in the 1830s, creating a powerful axis the other way towards the new custom house.

Castle Street, 1786, by Herdman.

West side Castle Street, 2006.

Most of the 1786 buildings were swept away during the following century to make Castle Street, one of the most sumptuous Victorian streets in Britain. So, it is difficult to imagine the street in Georgian times but we are given a tantalising glimpse by the survival of two buildings from that era, as can be seen in the present-day photo. The lower line of the Georgian buildings can be seen between the higher Victorian blocks. Above Brook Street's premises (No. 46) some sashed Georgian windows, the pilasters at each side, original stone surface and decorations have been retained. Nos 52–54 on the left have kept their white Georgian stucco, although bow windows have been added. The matching line of the cornices between the upper two storeys of both buildings hint at some uniformity of design along the street. The general disregard of Victorians for their Georgian heritage is highlighted by the insensitivity of Nos 48–50 towards its neighbours, in spite of being designed by Sir James Picton, an eminent Victorian architect. These have elaborate Classical and Romanesque excrescences and No. 44 on the right is better in this respect.

Greenbank

Greenbank is the remarkable home of a remarkable family. Built maybe fifty years earlier, it was first leased by the fourth William Rathbone in 1788. For many generations, the Rathbones, cultured and philanthropic, took a lead in the political and

Greenbank.

social life of the town. In 1784 'Rathbones' brought the first consignment of American cotton landed in England. In 1786 this William (a member of the Society of Friends) was one of only two Liverpool names to be on the list of the first members of the London Society for bringing to public notice the evils of the slave trade. His successor William was one of the seventeen leading reformers in the town who signed a notice to petition the Prince Regent and Parliament against suspension of the Habeas Corpus Act and later deploring the Peterloo massacre and supporting trade with China.

The original Georgian design of the main body of the house (visible in the foreshortened side to the left of the garden façade facing the viewer) was Gothicised around 1815 with a lace-like cast-iron structure over two storeys. This is typical of work in Liverpool at the time and it spread later through shipping trade to the Colonies and America. It is now a focal point of the Liverpool University Greenbank Student Village in Mossley Hill.

Blackburne House

When Blackburne House was built by John Blackburne around 1790 it was a detached mansion in the countryside. Falkner Street, which ran the other side of the wall at the rear, had originally been Crabtree Lane, a rural road that terminated in the fields. It was later renamed after the merchant family who had leased a large tract of the Mosslake Fields land from the Corporation for development. John Blackburne was Mayor of Liverpool in 1788 and enrolled a thousand men in one hour for the defence of Liverpool when a French invasion was threatened. His father, also John, had been mayor in 1760. It was an era when the Tory clique who ruled Liverpool ensured that their nominees were returned as Members of Parliament and, through the aldermanic system, many

Blackburne House.

a father and son or relative were elected mayor, sometimes twice, or, like John Foster father and son, appointed City Surveyor. The Blackburne family had previously lived in Hanover Street and the move gave them more space, privacy and peace. They made their money through trading in salt, which was produced in Cheshire and shipped to Africa. There it could be bartered for slaves and used in the West Indian and North American market. The house was of simple Georgian style, enhanced by a portico of four classical columns in Ionic form. Inside, a central staircase hall was lit by a domed skylight.

George Holt (Senior) bought the property in 1844 and converted it into Blackburne House School as a companion for the neighbouring Liverpool Institute. With later Victorian additions, it is now a women's training centre.

Heywood's Bank

The development of the Industrial Revolution in the north of England made increased credit facilities essential. Arthur Heywood, a merchant adventurer, came to Liverpool in 1731 and married into money. He and his brother Benjamin made a fortune out of the slave trade and took full advantage of the rich opportunities offered to Liverpool in the War of the Austrian Succession (1740–48). They were Unitarians who formed a significantly and increasingly influential group in Liverpool at the time and contributed to a number of good causes including the infirmary. Arthur played an important part in the literary scene. His expenditure on books was an important item and he chaired the meeting to found the Royal Institution. This aspiration to become cultured combined with the superior standard of dress of himself and his fellow bankers led to the expression 'Liverpool gentlemen' but 'Manchester men'. During the Seven Years

Above: Heywood's Bank.

Left: Heywood's Bank interior being converted.

War (1756–63) he prospered as a merchant banker, and during the War of American Independence (1775–83), he was lending money at higher rates of interest than those paid on deposits. The bank, the town and the country survived the financial pressures of the Napoleonic Wars (1793–1815).

The bank moved from its original premises In Castle Street into a new building, as shown, in Brunswick Street in 1800. An exceptionally early purpose-built bank, it has the Georgian characteristics of three storeys only, a plain cornice, sash windows without embellishments and a doorway with minimal classical adornment. Heywood's amalgamated with the Bank of Liverpool in 1883, which acquired and merged with Martin's Bank in 1918, bought by Barclays in 1969. The building became a branch when the magnificent new Martins Bank headquarters building by the Town Hall was opened in 1932. The interior photograph shows it being converted to other uses in 2006 when the beautiful Georgian decoration was being mutilated to adapt it to new uses.

Seymour Street

Seymour Street is a prime example of John Foster Senior's hand in the development of Liverpool's planned development. As town surveyor he saw the opportunity to extend northwards the ongoing building in Rodney Street. Having given himself planning permission, he secured a lease on the land, which was secured by business friends who sold half the land to himself. He then arranged for the land to be laid out and allotted to builders (possibly even himself). He was listed as an architect and so probably we owe to him the spaciousness of the elegant dwellings, which were in contrast to the surrounding cramped houses and gardens. Two rainwater heads dated 1810 and 1823 indicate the progress of the development completed in 1826, by which time land values had increased between two and three times in the streets involved. This conflict of interest would not be countenanced today, although Foster does not seem to have profited exorbitantly or illegally out of it.

In 1984 the whole terrace was in a state of ruin. Since then, the façades have been restored with iron balconies and railings. However, individual variations in appearance of doorways and fanlights have been standardised to provide office accommodation behind as indicated by the plaques. The wedge lintels to the sashed windows are as originals.

Seymour Street terrace.

Doorcases

The variety of doorcases (the surround of the door) is an attractive feature of Georgian houses. They provided the opportunity to show off your individuality and importance, welcoming you home and impressing your visitors. The solid door, usually with

Top left: No. 150 Chatham Street.

Top right: No. 13 Canning Street.

Bottom left: Huskisson Street.

Bottom right: No. 8 Percy Street.

six panels, could be embellished with a classical column on each side. This could be fully rounded or squared, or half engaged (attached) to the wall or flat shaped (a pilaster). The most common form was the Doric, fluted (with vertical grooves) or plain (sometimes known as the Tuscan or Roman Doric form). The top of the column might be decorated with rings and a square slab (No. 150 Chatham Street) and over it, a pattern of triglyphs (three grooves) with a plain or decorated panel between them known as metopes (Nos 16–24 Falkner Street) The Ionic order sported scrolls on the capital (top) of the column (Huskisson Street and No. 13 Canning Street). The more elaborate Corinthian capital would be decorated with a flower decoration (in its purest form, acanthus leaves) and be combined with an Ionic scroll to form the Composite order (No. 8 Percy Street). The door was surmounted by a fanlight, rectangular or semicircular, to let light into the hall. It might be decorated by geometric shapes with glazing bars. The 'rubber' bricks round a semicircular fanlight might be shaped to form an embracing arch (Nos 16–24 Falkner Street). The other bricks were usually laid in a 'Flemish' bond with alternate full bricks and half bricks. The second storey rooms often displayed iron balconies with intricate designs but these were for decorative purposes only. Many of them have been added or restored recently. At roof level triangular pediments, sometimes with internal decoration, created the impression of an ancient Greek temple.

No. 24 Falkner Street.

Abercromby Square

In 1800 the Corporation approved plans drawn up by John Foster Senior, the Corporation Surveyor, for the development of Mosslake Fields. The focal point was Abercromby Square, named after Sir Ralph Abercromby, the general killed at Alexandria in 1801. A grid pattern of streets was to be laid out, which extends from the square and can be seen to this day in Bedford Street, Chatham Street and the blocks in between. Abercromby Square is the only complete block at the top of Swire's 1823/4 map (orientated from the west) with the fields to the right soon to be developed on a similar grid pattern to include Percy Street and Canning Street. Prominent just below the Square to the left is the House of Industry (workhouse) with the House of Recovery above it and almshouses to its right (soon to be replaced by the Medical Institution). At the bottom of the map, Rodney Street, Liverpool's pioneer Georgian style housing, leads to the quarry, soon to be transformed into St James' cemetery.

Plots in Abercromby Square were sold to conform individually to a high standard of superior housing. The square presented a uniform and balanced appearance as a

Moss Lake Fields area from Swire's map, 1823–24.

Abercromby Square terrace.

whole. In the middle of one side stood St Catherine's Church with imposing Ionic columns; the other sides had a prominent projecting doorway to mark the centre point with classical columns of the Doric order. In this way individuality was preserved and this was combined with mutual harmony, the hallmark of the Georgian style. Balconies embellished with ornate ironwork followed the latest fashion. There was a semi basement with steps up to a solid front door, designed to be a defence against possible aggressive rioters who would be faced with the equivalent of a moat and uphill attack over a drawbridge.

The houses surrounded a garden square that was guarded by a fence with locked gates. Entry could only be gained by subscribers with a key or by non-residents who paid a fee. This park provided the residents with a pleasant view from their windows and a sense of security and separation from the surrounding area (the workhouse, for example). Social events and entertainments such as concerts were organised. The lawn, paths and bedding were looked after by gardeners who could store their tools in the delightful structure illustrated. To the left of the photo is the only modern structure surrounding the square. It is the Senate House, which has replaced St Catharine's Church, built by John Foster Junior in 1831 but demolished after suffering bomb

Left: Abercromby Square fortified entrance.

Below: Abercromby Square garden house.

damage In the Second World War. Otherwise, the buildings are as built from around 1816 to 1830 and the basic pattern of streets has been preserved to this day. They are all now part of the university precinct.

Percy Street Terrace West Side

St Bride's Church in Percy Street is accompanied by two magnificent terraces that together contribute to one of the finest architectural streets in Liverpool, superior to its namesake in London. On the west side, as pictured, there is a perfect balance between the two houses with pediments. The one to the left has its pedimented window off centre to the right of the portico but in the distance, the door is on the right (as in the detailed photo below). The centre point between these two houses is marked by a portico with three columns instead of two for all the others.

It is worth examining and appreciating the façade of one of these houses in detail since it is as lavishly decorated as any in the country. Starting from the top, the triangular pediment is flanked by two acroteria (ornamental decorations) in palmette

Percy Street west terrace.

Percy Street west terrace house façade.

(palm tree) form and enhanced by a wreath in the centre. As you move down, the windowpanes conform to a pattern often used in Georgian terraces: the top storey has the least number, in this case, 3x1 over 3x2 (sometimes elsewhere 3x1 over 3x1); the middle storey is the most impressive, often, as here, 3x2 over 3x3; the ground level, less so, has on the left a common configuration of 3x2 over 3x2 but the superior house in the centre has, most unusually, an impressive 4x2 over 4x2. The embellishment of the windows varies similarly. On the top storey of the standard house on the left, they are set back in simple frames, while on the middle storey, they have panelled frames with palmettes in the top corners similar to the ground floor. The architect displays his full classical repertoire on the ground floor of the show house: a pediment is supported by scrolls modelled on the Erechtheum on the Acropolis in Athens with palmettes emblazoned on the scrolls, panelled framing and corner wreaths. The ironwork of the balcony is finely wrought with appropriate tracery. The columns in pilaster form also increase in glory as the eye moves down. Paired on a small scale on the top storey, the two lower stories are embraced by gigantic columns.

Wreaths hang on the lintels over the columns, almost resting on lion's heads incorporated in the capitals of the columns below. The decoration of the capitals is intricate and idiosyncratic. Ionic scrolls part to enclose lotus flowers, Corinthian acanthus leaves create a Composite order and a palmette and egg and dart pattern completes the ensemble. The doorway reflects in miniature the design of the whole. From top to bottom in the detailed photo are a palmette, acroterion, wreath and Ionic scrolls, accompanied by a rosette and honeysuckle.

Above left: Percy Street detail of column capital.

Above right: Percy Street detail of door frame.

Percy Street east terrace.

Percy Street Terrace East Side

Like its companion on the opposite side, the terrace is decorated lavishly in classical style. A grand portico is stepped forward to mark the centre point with an iron balustrade above. This enables a Doric colonnade to connect with the end houses also standing proud to form pavilions with corner acroteria to harmonise with the others. The first-floor windows are larger than those on the ground floor (3+2 panes in height compared with 2+2). They combine with the iron balconies to draw attention to the main suite of rooms on the first floor (like the piano nobile of an Italian palazzo).

St Bride's Church

The best surviving neoclassical church in the city also contains the monument of a tragedy typical of an almost annual event, and more, in the reign of the Georges. A memorial to W. M. Forster, his wife and servant record their drowning in a wreck of the Rothesay Castle. She was a paddle steamer constructed on the River Clyde in 1816 where she plied until 1831 when she was bought by a Liverpool businessman for the North Wales service. However, she was underpowered, and in a bad state of repair, as was her only lifeboat. Her sailing was delayed by poor weather and the late arrival of Mr Forster's coach, which caused further delay because of difficulties getting it aboard. The intoxicated captain refused to turn back when the ship battled against the wind and tide near the Menai Straits where she foundered. Only 23 out of the 150 on board were saved.

St Bride's style and materials fit in perfectly with the surrounding Georgian terraces. The general appearance is of a Greek temple, as with many other fashionable

St Bride's Church.

churches of the period elsewhere, with six columns ('hexastyle', as so often) of the Ionic order. Unusually, entrance is by two doors with a central window. The six (also) windows down the side are richly decorated with scrolls on each side at the top that are modelled on the Erechtheion on the Acropolis in Athens. The windows at each end are flanked by giant pilasters and framed with anthemion (flower) decorations at the top.

Mount Street

An unusual Georgian terrace without balance or overall design has grown along Hope Street. The four bays of No. 35 Mount Street on the left contribute two bays on the return to the façade along Hope Street, which is composed of four houses each of three bays. The first two are three storeys in height followed by a superior looking two-storey bowed house (rare in Georgian Liverpool) in the centre with a heavy cornice at the top adding an imposing focal point. A two-storey lower block then completes the variety. Behind the doorway of No. 35 Mount Street a Georgian staircase leads up to the first floor. Natural light is shed through the fanlight during the day and a chandelier (lit in Georgian times by oil or candle) supplies illumination at night.

Hope/Mount Street terrace.

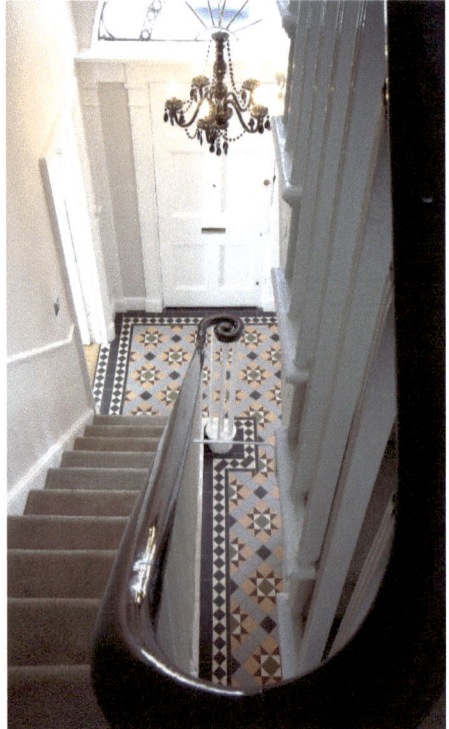

Above left: No. 35 Mount Street door.

Above right: No. 35 Mount Street staircase.

Nos 167/9 Bedford Street South and Nos 25–51 Huskisson Street.

Huskisson Street

Sixteen identical Ionic porticos grace the symmetrical terrace. All of them lead to a house of three bays except at each end where they are projected forward with five and four bays to give the impression of pavilions and a superior finish to the ensemble. Ground and first-storey sashed windows have stone wedge lintels with glazing bars.

Falkner Terrace

The terrace (in Upper Parliament Street) is a perfect example of Georgian architecture's principles of balance, simplicity and subtle variation of emphasis in adornment. Tuscan pilasters (squared columns attached to the walls) decorate the paired doorways (single

Falkner Terrace, Nos 155–177 Upper Parliament Street.

at each end). They also appear between the first-floor windows of the projecting end and centre houses, which sport iron balconies. The second-floor windows (sashed with glazing bars) are set in recessed panels. The windowpanes follow a pattern often used in Georgian terraces: on the ground floor 3x2 over 3x2; first floor 3x2 over 3x3 to give added impressiveness and the second floor 3x1 over 3x1 to lend diminished importance to the 'attic storey'. The walls of the stucco façade are grouted at ground level to simulate masonry (known as rustication).

The terrace, started in 1831 and predating the nearby Falkner Square, stood isolated for so long it was known as 'Falkner's Folly'. It was restored by TACP Architects in 1986.

Canning Street

The exquisite precision of balance in the design of this Georgian-style terrace is remarkable. The porticoes are in Ionic style with the columns in pairs except for those beneath the two pediments. A row of porticoes with columns forms the entrances to the houses. The monotony of two columns is broken up by two three-columned

Nos 18–50 Canning Street.

porticos positioned below the pediments at the roof level. These are accompanied by a third midway between them. The block projects forward beneath the pediments.

Gambier Terrace

Gambier Terrace was a final flourish of the Georgian period in Liverpool. Although technically it comes within the reign of William IV, there is no recognised style of that short period and Liverpool tended to be behind London (and Bath in this instance) in architectural fashion. In fact, the Georgian style continued to be employed into Victoria's reign. The terrace occupied a most desirable residential site with open views over the landscaped St James' cemetery, the town and River Mersey to the Wirral and Welsh hills beyond. Started in the early 1830s on such a grand scale that it was not completed for another forty years, the prime development was stopped because of the slump of 1837 and the decline in demand for new city houses as the affluent travelled by rail to new suburbs. The unknown architect emphasised the monumental scale by the use of ashlar and stucco, materials that are used to great effect in imitating a rustic base. In addition, giant fully rounded Ionic columns span two floors above a projecting

Gambier Terrace.

Greek Doric porch, also completely formed. Columns like this in Georgian houses are not often found even in London and Bath. The rounded (Venetian) windows, rare in Liverpool, are a statement of wealth and status. Entrance through the porch leads you to a grand hall with a towering staircase leading to a domed roof. The doorway at the end of Gambier Terrace facing onto Canning Street (No. 2) is a companion in Doric style to the one that faces onto Hope Street that can be seen in the previous image, only the columns are half rounded against the wall instead of fully rounded.

No. 2 Canning Street, Gambier Terrace.